Quick Guide to "You've Got Pictures"℠

David Peal

Quick Guide to "You've Got Pictures"℠

Published by
America Online, Inc.
22000 AOL Way
Dulles, VA 20166
www.aol.com (America Online Web site)

Library of Congress Control Number:

ISBN: 0-7645-3527-7

1O/SQ/QZ/QQ/IN

Printed in the United States by America Online, Inc.

Credits

America Online

Cover Design:
DKG Design, Inc

IDG Books Worldwide

Acquisitions and Editorial

Editors:
Nicole Haims
Kim Darosett,
Rebecca Senninger

Acquisitions Editor:
Kathy Yankton

Editorial Manager:
Leah Cameron

Publishing Director:
Andy Cummings

Production

Project Coordinator:
Tony Augsburger

Layout and Graphics:
Kelly Hardesty
LeAndra Johnson
Brian Torwelle

Proofreader:
Brian Massey

Indexer:
Sharon Hilgenberg

Navigating Through This Book

Check out the Table of Contents or each chapter's introductory bullets for an overview of chapter contents. Try the Index if you're looking for something specific. And please see the following sections for information on helpful conventions that we use throughout the book.

Web Addresses and Menu Selections

The address of Web sites will show up in a different font, as follows: `www.photoalley.com`. Also, the ⇨ symbol indicates menu selections. For example, Sign Off⇨Switch Screen Name tells you to click the Sign Off menu on the AOL menu bar and choose Switch Screen Name from the drop-down menu.

Icons

We call your attention to important concepts and information throughout the book by using the following icons:

Tip — Tips provide you with extra knowledge that separates the novice from the pro.

Note — Notes provide additional or critical information and technical data on the current topic.

Definition — Definitions explain terms and concepts.

Find It Online — Find It Online icons direct you to a location on AOL or the Internet.

Caution — Caution icons give you information to help you avoid frustration.

Table of Contents

Chapter 1

Introducing "You've Got Pictures"℠

In This Chapter

- Finding and touring the "You've Got Pictures" service
- Getting your pictures online
- Sharing your pictures with friends and family
- Turning your pictures into prints and gifts
- Looking over the whole Picture Community
- Looking at safety considerations

What microcomputers and word-processing software did to the world of *text* in the 1980s, digital-imaging equipment (like digital cameras and scanners) and the Internet are doing right now to the world of *photographs.* With the "You've Got Pictures" service, online leader America Online and Kodak have created an easy-to-use service for collecting, storing, and sharing pictures online. This book introduces you to the many exciting features of "You've Got Pictures."

Finding "You've Got Pictures" on the Welcome Screen

America Online gives you easy access to the "You've Got Pictures" service. For starters, you'll find its icon right on the AOL Welcome Screen, as shown in Figure 1-1. Click this icon to go to the "You've Got Pictures" online area. As always, AOL gives you choices about how you interact with its online services. You can also use any of the following AOL keywords to get to "You've Got Pictures."

- AOL Keyword: **Pictures**
- AOL Keyword: **YGP**
- AOL Keyword: **You've Got Pictures**

"You've Got Pictures" icon

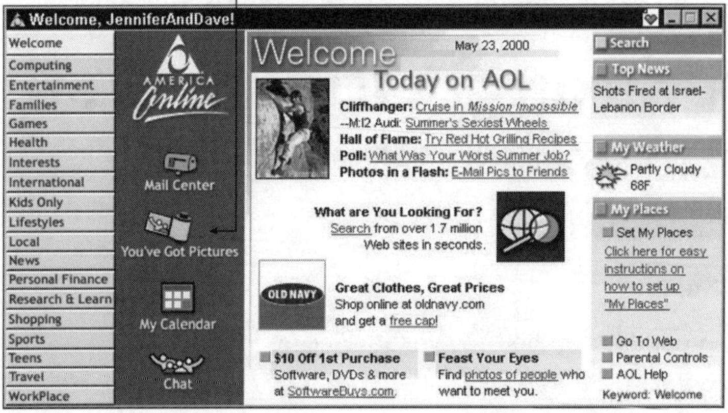

Figure 1-1. You can access "You've Got Pictures" right from the AOL Welcome Screen.

What You Can Do with Digital Pictures

With its "You've Got Pictures" service, AOL is your central location for anything you might want to do with online pictures. You can stuff your pictures in an e-mail "envelope," pass around electronic photo albums, emblazon gift items with your images, and display your pictures in electronic photo galleries. Here's a brief overview of what you can do:

- **E-mail.** This is the easiest way to pass around your digital pictures. "You've Got Pictures" has its own, easy-to-use system for e-mailing individual pictures, and AOL's regular e-mail features make sending your own pictures a snap. If you send e-mail to AOL members, you can include the pictures in the body of the e-mail — no files to download or links to click!
- **Albums.** Why send individual pictures when you can assemble photo albums that nearly anyone with Internet access can display? With Buddy Albums, you can organize and share your favorite moments with one person, or dozens.
- **On AOL.** America Online offers members many ways to share their pictures with each other. You can upload your image files to libraries, enter your pictures in contests, and share them in online galleries.

- **Products based on digital pictures.** "You've Got Pictures" can take your digital photos and turn them into quality prints and enlargements, and put them on mugs, sweatshirts, and teddy bears, to add a whole new dimension to gift giving. Figure 1-2 shows you what's available at the "You've Got Pictures" store.
- **The Web.** If want to share your photos with an even bigger audience, you may prefer to put them on a Web page. Let "You've Got Pictures" do the processing and add the results to your home page.

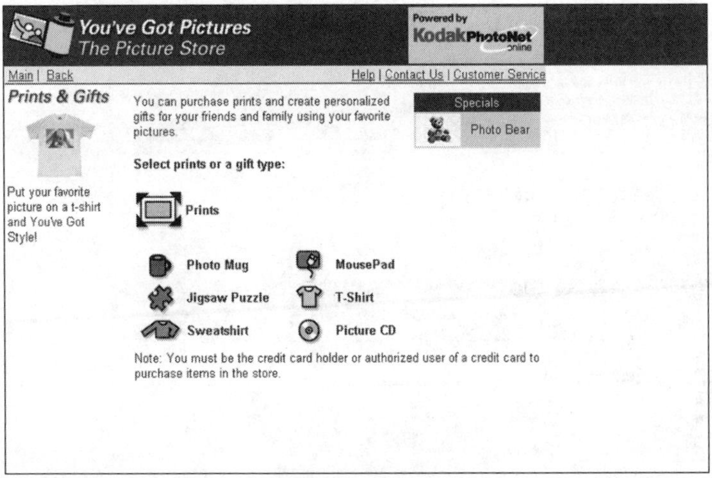

Figure 1-2. The Picture Store offers prints and gifts.

A Quick Tour of the "You've Got Pictures" Service

The cornerstone of AOL's digital-imaging initiatives is the online service area called "You've Got Pictures" (AOL Keyword: **Pictures**). When you access "You've Got Pictures" for the first time, you see the main page shown in Figure 1-3. After you have pictures developed and delivered or uploaded to the service, you see the My Pictures page shown in Figure 1-4. Here's where you start building your online collection of digital pictures.

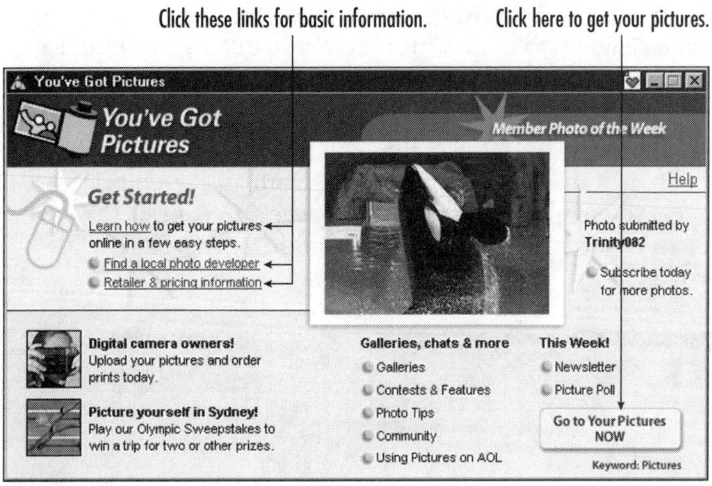

Figure 1-3. The "You've Got Pictures" main page.

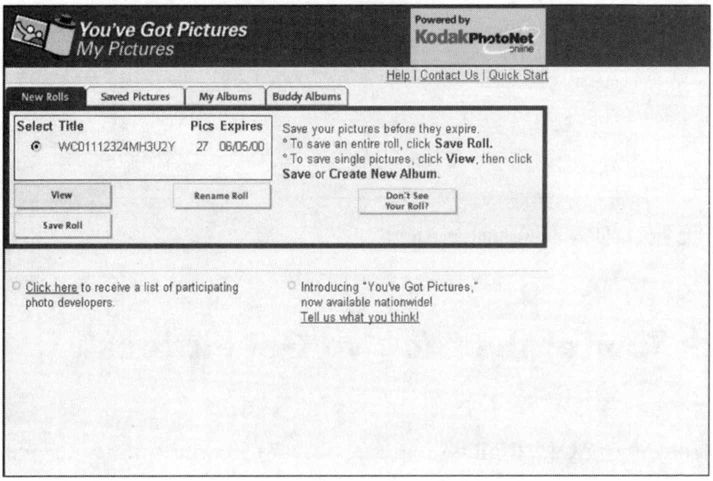

Figure 1-4. Start here to view, share, organize, and store your digital pictures.

Click the Learn How link from the "You've Got Pictures" main page to discover the easy steps for getting your pictures online. You can also click the Quick Start link from the My Pictures page to find the same helpful information on using all the "You've Got Pictures" features.

Getting Your Film to a Participating Developer

From the main "You've Got Pictures" page, you can find out the location of participating photo developers in your area. Click the Find a Local Photo Developer link from the main page (see Figure 1-3) or the Click Here link from the My Pictures page (see Figure 1-4). In either case, you'll be prompted to enter location information (like your zip code) so that "You've Got Pictures" can supply you with a listing of participating photo developers in your area.

To get digital pictures on your AOL account, you just check the AOL box on the film processing envelope and provide an AOL screen name when you drop off your film at a participating retailer (most large drugstores and supermarkets are members). Refer to Chapter 2 for more information on finding and using "You've Got Pictures" processors.

Getting Your New Rolls

Picking up your rolls online is a snap with "You've Got Pictures." After you find a participating developer and drop off your film, your processed pictures are delivered to your AOL account under the screen name you provided. Sign on to AOL using that screen name, and you may be delighted to hear the greeting "You've got pictures!" Go to "You've Got Pictures" (AOL Keyword: **Pictures**) and get ready to look for your new roll. Chapter 2 gives you specifics about finding and viewing your pictures online.

Note

After you drop off your film, your pictures should be uploaded and online within 48 hours. If you drop off your roll at a participating one-hour photo lab, your pictures may be online in a matter of hours.

Uploading Your Pictures from a Digital Camera or Scanner

Suppose that you already have digital pictures on your computer. They may be pictures that someone else shared with you, or pictures you've scanned, or pictures you've taken with a digital camera — it doesn't really matter how you get them. If you're signed on to AOL, you can copy them (upload them) directly from your computer to "You've Got Pictures." See Chapter 4 for more information about uploading.

Definition

Uploading is the term commonly used for transferring an electronic document or picture from one computer to another, usually from a personal computer to an Internet-connected computer, sometimes called a *server* (AOL has about a zillion such computers), where many people can view the document or picture.

Sharing Your Pictures through E-mail

Think of how you share photographic prints: You can show them to people, one person at a time. Or you can get duplicates or reprints and mail them to grandparents and whoever else might be interested. With "You've Got Pictures," you can send an individual picture to anyone with an e-mail account, as well as include an electronic greeting or write a few words about your picture. Your picture and message arrive in the recipient's electronic mailbox (just the way you receive your e-mail).

See Chapter 3 for step-by-step instructions on how to share your online pictures through e-mail and see Figure 1-5 for a view of a picture shared this way.

Saving and Storing Pictures Online

It's important to realize that your digital pictures have two homes, that is, two places where you can store them, share them, and create things with them. These two places are "You've Got Pictures" and your own PC. Saving the pictures that you had developed and delivered to your AOL account is as simple as clicking a button on the My Pictures page.

And the "You've Got Pictures" service comes with space for storing your pictures online for free. See Chapter 4 for more information on saving and storing your pictures online.

Creating and Sharing Buddy Albums

Another fun way of sharing your pictures is by creating and sharing photo albums with your friends and family. With "You've Got Pictures," you can create and share online albums that contain your digital pictures. Click the My Albums tab and follow the simple instructions in Chapter 5 to create and share your own Buddy Albums.

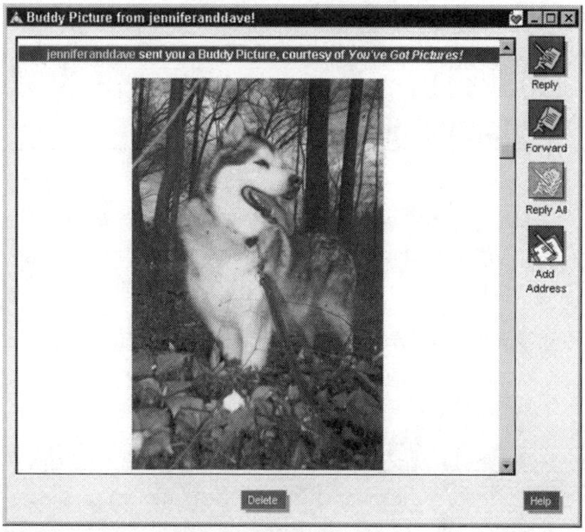

Figure 1-5. A picture worth sharing.

Turning Your Pictures into Prints and Gifts

The uses for online pictures are endless. Gift giving is one of the more popular uses, and certainly one of the easier uses, thanks to the photo gifts available online directly through "You've Got Pictures."

Note Pictures gifts are available through "You've Got Pictures" for AOL members and non-AOL members alike. That is, non-AOL members can order picture gifts featuring the Buddy Album photographs that they've received from AOL members.

"You've Got Pictures" makes ordering gifts easy. Look for the Order Prints & Gifts button when you view pictures in the New Rolls, Saved Pictures, or albums tabs, and make your selections in the "You've Got Pictures" Picture Store. See Chapter 7 for step-by-step instructions.

Exploring the Picture Community with "You've Got Pictures"

The "You've Got Pictures" main page is the center of an online community built around sharing digital pictures. The main page gives you links to information that helps you get started with the "You've Got Pictures" service, promotes community spirit by showing you the Member Photo of the Week, and leads you to an array of other online activities (contests, chats, newsletters, and more). To reach the main page (shown in Figure 1-3), go to AOL Keyword: **Picture Community**.

The following table lists some of the various features, information, and activities that are available from the "You've Got Pictures" main page.

Main Page Feature	What It Does
Learn How link	Opens the "You've Got Pictures" Quick Start (see Figure 1-6) with the View, Share, and Order tabs that explain the basic elements of the service
Find a Local Photo Developer link	Opens the window that prompts you to enter location information and find a participating photo developer in your area
Retailer & Pricing Information link	Opens a window with general dealer and pricing information and additional links to answer frequently asked questions
Galleries option	Opens the Photo Galleries window with links to photo areas related to sports, news, and many other interests
Contests & Features option	Opens the Contests & Features window with links to sweepstakes, photo contests, special albums, and other features
Photo Tips option	Opens the Photo Tips window with links to product reviews, discussions with photo hobbyists, and expert advice on taking photos
Community option	Opens the Community Page with links to chats, forums, message boards, and the *Picture This!* newsletter (see Figure 1-7)
Newsletter option	Opens to This Week's Newsletter with links for subscribing to *Picture This!*, the official "You've Got Pictures" newsletter
Picture Poll option	Opens to the Picture Poll question of the week and links to previous polls and a message board for suggesting a picture poll question

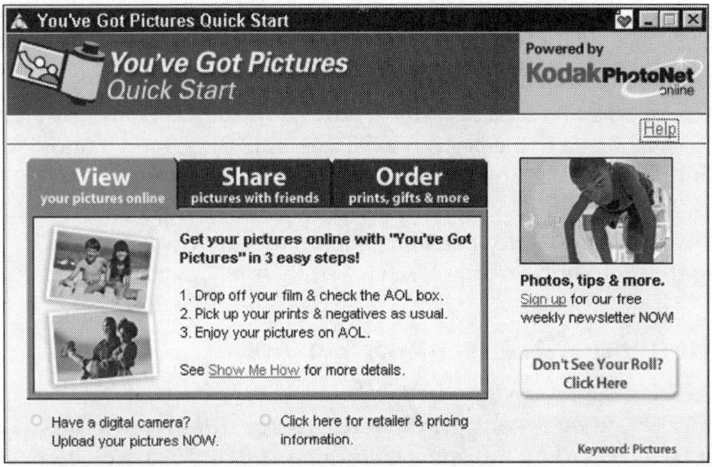

Figure 1-6. Get started with "You've Got Pictures" by using the Quick Start.

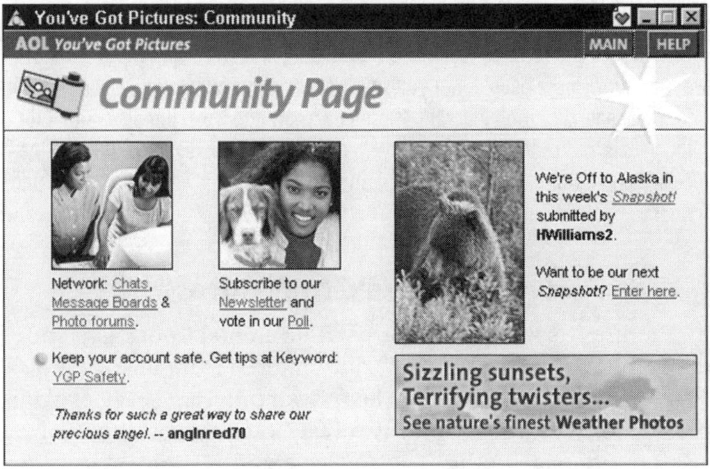

Figure 1-7. Get in touch with fellow photographers on the Community Page.

Safety Considerations

America Online has a well-deserved reputation for providing a safe and secure online environment, and "You've Got Pictures" has been made safe for minors. In fact, the service is available only for screen names that are set up with the Mature Teen (16-17) or General Access (18+) age groups. "You've Got Pictures" provides a thorough discussion of online safety and security issues in its Help area, which you can reach by clicking the Help link on any "You've Got Pictures" page.

Understanding AOL's Terms of Service

"You've Got Pictures" is covered by AOL's Terms of Service (TOS), which governs members' conduct on AOL. "You've Got Pictures" has its own set of rules regarding the special conditions that can arise when using and exchanging digital pictures. In addition to the usual prohibitions of sexually explicit, obscene, and defamatory material, "You've Got Pictures" has rules regarding issues such as soliciting business and violating copyright laws.

Note

The "You've Got Pictures" service is a confidentially secure space, just like AOL e-mail. Only those people that you specify can access your pictures, allowing you to safely share your albums with those you know and trust. But understand that the people you share your pictures with can also download your pictures to their own "You've Got Pictures" space and, in turn, share them with their friends and family.

Keeping Kids Safe at "You've Got Pictures"

"You've Got Pictures" is integrated with AOL's Parental Controls, a special feature that allows you to protect your children from unsolicited, inappropriate images and to prevent them from ordering services without your permission. For more about Parental Controls, you can read the Safety & Security page in the "You've Got Pictures" Help area.

Note

Kids Only and Young Teens screen names do not have access to AOL Keyword: **Pictures.**

Visit AOL Keywords: **Parental Controls** and **Community Watch** to learn of the many ways you can protect your children online.

Secure Commerce

AOL makes online commerce safe, easy, and reliable. "You've Got Pictures" is part of AOL's Certified Merchants program, which guarantees the safety of your credit card information and sets stringent standards for customer support and accountability to consumers.

Privacy

AOL matches the screen name that you provide to "You've Got Pictures" (when you drop off your film) with your address and telephone number. This security measure ensures that a simple error doesn't send your pictures to the wrong person.

Chapter 2

Getting Your Pictures Online

In This Chapter

- Locating a participating photo developer
- Taking your film to be developed
- Picking up your pictures online
- Uploading your scanned or digital camera photos into "You've Got Pictures"
- Viewing and renaming your online pictures

From cradle to grave, life is enhanced with photographs. About as soon as the cord is cut, most newborn babies are captured in a snapshot with a happy mom or proud dad. And although the path from traditional pictures to digital (online) pictures may seem daunting, it's actually direct and not particularly thorny. The material in this chapter tells you how to get your pictures online, how to pick them up there, and how to work with them a bit through AOL's "You've Got Pictures" service.

Finding a Participating "You've Got Pictures" Dealer

The "You've Got Pictures" service is supported by 38,000 dealers, including most locations offering Kodak processing, 1-hour labs like Wolf Camera, and leading mail order photofinishers. The next time you take in your film to be developed, look for a sign that the dealer offers "You've Got Pictures." Also, you can find a participating developer by following a link from the "You've Got Pictures" main page, shown in Figure 2-1.

Click here to locate a photo developer.

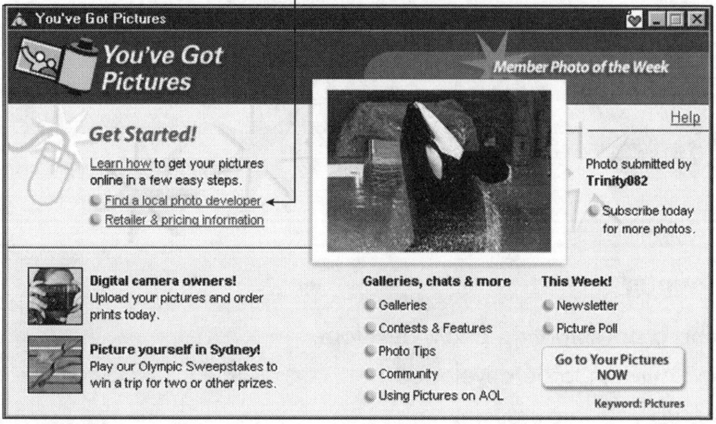

Figure 2-1. The "You've Got Pictures" main page.

Tip: The "You've Got Pictures" service works with any brand of 35mm color print film, single-use cameras, and APS (Advanced Photo System) film.

Why not let your mouse do the walking, though? "You've Got Pictures" maintains a complete list of participating dealers at AOL Keyword: **Photo Developer**, or you can click the handy blue hyperlink on the "You've Got Pictures" main page (AOL Keyword: **Picture Community**). Using AOL Keyword: **Photo Developer** takes you to the Photo Developer Dealer Locator, shown in Figure 2-2.

With about 38,000 dealers on that list, AOL makes it easy to find photo developers in your own backyard. Follow these steps:

1. Go to AOL Keyword: **Photo Developer**.
2. Type your city and state, or zip code, or your area code and the first three digits of your phone number in the Enter Location text box.
3. Click the Find button and you receive a listing of "You've Got Pictures" dealers in your area, as shown in Figure 2-3.

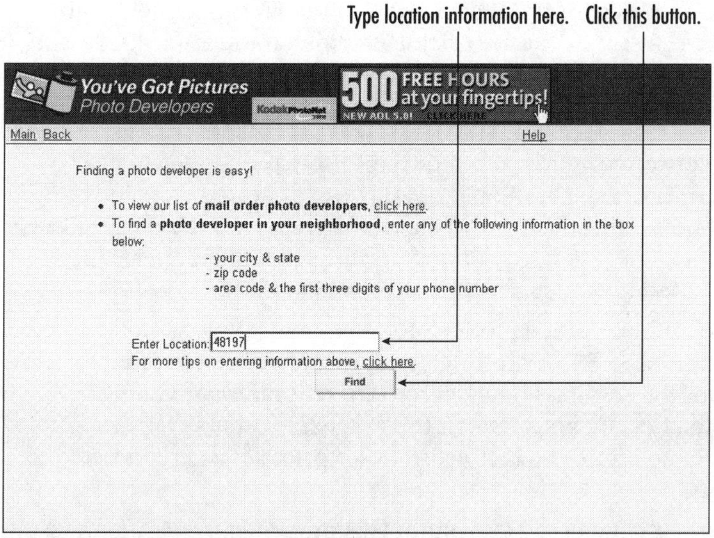

Figure 2-2. The Photo Developer Dealer Locator.

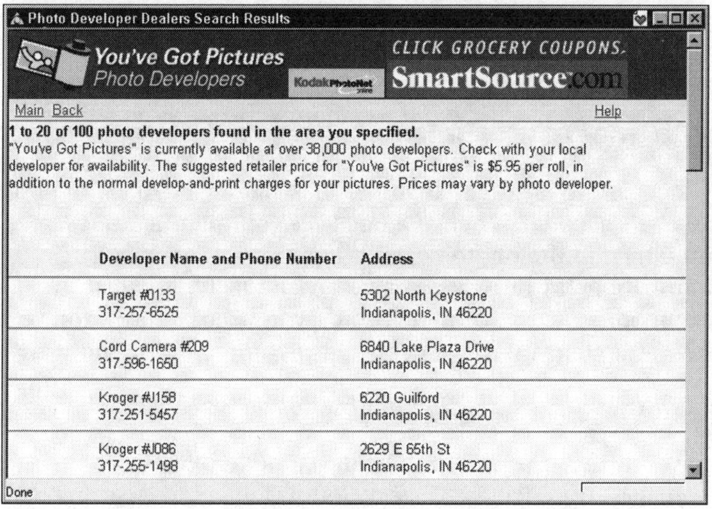

Figure 2-3. Find your local dealer that offers "You've Got Pictures."

If your area has more than 20 participating dealers, click the Next button at the bottom of the list to see more listings (up to 100 in all). Regardless of whether your search turns up 100 dealers or none at all, you'll find a new Enter Location box at the bottom of the page, which makes it easy to try again.

AOL also provides a listing of mail-order photo labs that offer "You've Got Pictures." Just look for the Click Here link on the Photo Developer Dealer Locator page. Here are a few points to consider when choosing a photo processor:

- **Convenience.** AOL's photo dealers' list makes finding a nearby dealer very easy. On the page listing the photo retailers in your neighborhood, or the empty page if there are no nearby retailers, click the Mail Order Photo Developers link for alternative, mail-in services such as Mystic Color Lab and York Photo.
- **Price.** Although the recommended price for "You've Got Pictures" is $5.95 per roll, dealers can and do charge more or less for the service. Some charge different rates depending on the number of exposures on the roll, while others charge a flat rate. Some require that you also order prints of a certain size or quality.
- **Range of services.** Most photo labs process only 35mm or Advantix print films and disposable cameras. Some labs offer additional services, including scans of 35mm slides, existing 35mm negatives, or even copies of old prints. If you need these extra services, it pays to make a few phone calls.

Making Sure Your Pictures Arrive Online

AOL has a safeguard to ensure that your online pictures don't show up in someone else's account. When AOL receives your pictures, the screen name you supplied to the photo dealer is compared to your AOL account information. If your screen name doesn't match the name and telephone number in AOL's account records, you will not hear "You've got pictures" (although you can access your pictures an alternate way).

Here are a few ways to ensure that your photos do reach you:

- Before you bring in your film to be developed, go to AOL Keyword: **Billing**, click the Change Your Name or Address link, and update your account information (only screen names with Master rights can access and change billing info).
- Be sure that the name, phone number, and screen name you give to the photo lab matches the information you supplied to AOL Billing.
- Double-check all the information you supplied. All you have to do now is wait!

Note When the pictures are delivered to your AOL account, you receive an e-mail message from the screen name `AOL YouveGotPics`, indicating how to access your pictures. In addition, if you have AOL 5.0 for Windows, the "You've Got Pictures" icon on the main AOL Welcome Screen changes from an empty film cannister to one with a piece of film coming out of it, and a familiar voice announces "You've got pictures!" Click the icon or use AOL Keyword: **Pictures** to view your new roll.

Dropping Off Your Film

You can drop off your film at most major supermarkets and large drugstores, or mail it in to many of the popular mail-order photofinishers.

Whenever you drop off your film, ask for the "You've Got Pictures" service and check the AOL check box on the film processing envelope, shown in Figure 2-4. Then write in your AOL screen name; otherwise, the processor won't know where to send your digital pictures when they're finished. Your AOL account can have up to seven screen names, and you can send your pictures to nearly any screen name you choose.

Note Screen names with Parental Controls set to Kids Only or Young Teens cannot access "You've Got Pictures."

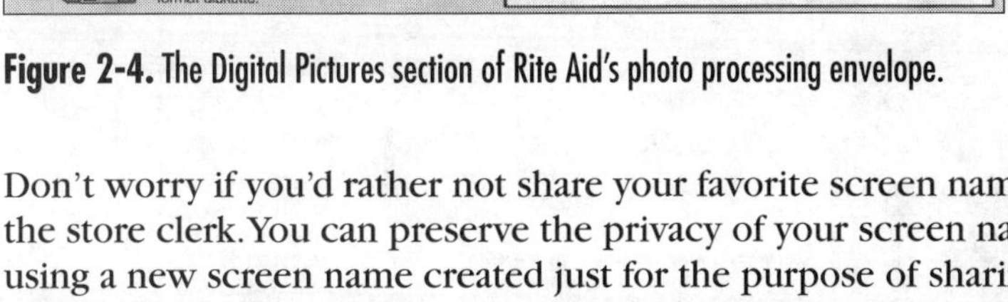

Figure 2-4. The Digital Pictures section of Rite Aid's photo processing envelope.

Don't worry if you'd rather not share your favorite screen name with the store clerk. You can preserve the privacy of your screen name by using a new screen name created just for the purpose of sharing pictures or by not supplying a screen name at all. As you'll see in the next section, you can access your pictures by using the Roll ID and Owner's Key, which you receive when you pick up your prints from the store.

Picking Up Your Pictures Online

Waiting was sometimes the hardest part of traditional (film) photography. Many questions plague you between taking your pictures and getting the prints. Did the camera work? Are the exposures good? What about that wonderful sunset over the water or those precious shots of your retriever chasing the ducks?

Tip Some one-hour photo labs can do all the developing right on the premises — they have scanning equipment that sends the digital images straight to "You've Got Pictures." Bring in your film, return in one hour for your prints and negatives, and your digital pictures may be online before you get home!

Developing film used to mean dashing down to your favorite photo processor and dropping off your film. And waiting. "You've Got Pictures" can save you all this waiting around because picking up your (digital) pictures is just about as easy as getting your e-mail.

Sign on to America Online, go to "You've Got Pictures," and with a couple of clicks (see the "Viewing Your Pictures" section), you're looking at your pictures! Just to make sure, AOL also sends you e-mail notification that your pictures have arrived. Right below the mailbox icon on your AOL Welcome Screen is the "You've Got Pictures" icon, which has a colorful little picture emerging from that film cannister when you receive your pictures, as shown in Figure 2-5.

"You've Got Pictures" icon

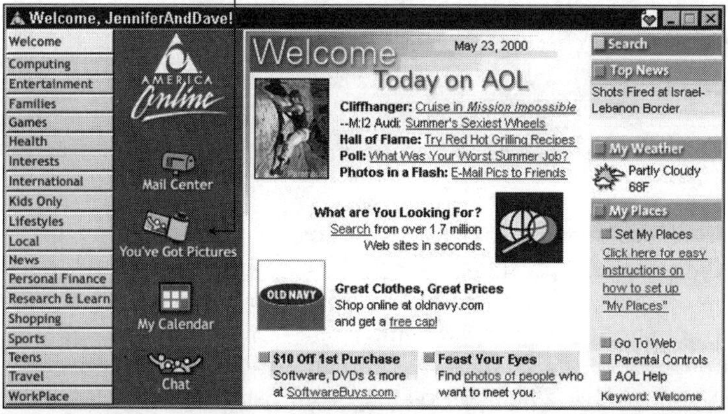

Figure 2-5. If your digital pictures have arrived, you hear "Welcome! You've got pictures!" when you sign on.

Viewing Your Pictures

Viewing your pictures online is the equivalent of tearing open the envelope containing your brand-new prints. First, you have to sign on to AOL with the screen name you gave to the photo lab. After you're connected to AOL, click the "You've Got Pictures" icon on the AOL Welcome Screen (see Figure 2-5), or use *any* of the following AOL keywords to access "You've Got Pictures":

- **YGP**
- **You've Got Pictures**
- **Pictures**

Near the top of the "You've Got Pictures" page, shown in Figure 2-6, you find four *tabs* (which are sort of like the index tabs in a notebook): New Rolls, Saved Pictures, My Albums, and Buddy Albums. For now, focus on the New Rolls tab. If it isn't already selected, click the New Rolls tab to display the New Rolls page. If you have a roll (or rolls) waiting for you, the New Rolls page displays automatically.

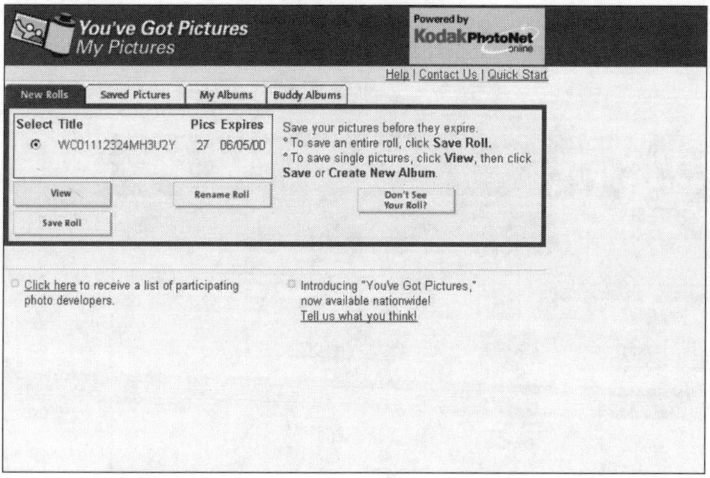

Figure 2-6. The "You've Got Pictures" New Rolls tab, showing a new roll of pictures.

Every new roll of pictures that you receive is stored on "You've Got Pictures" for 30 days. Listed next to each roll is a title, the number of exposures, and the expiration date of that roll. Any images that you don't save by the end of that 30-day period are deleted, just as old e-mail is deleted from your online mailbox.

Viewing a Roll

Right below the list of new rolls are four buttons — View, Rename Roll, Don't See Your Roll, and Save Roll. The first thing you want to do is view your new pictures. To do so, make sure to click inside the circle (so that it's selected) next to the roll you want to view and click View. Within moments the Roll Viewer page opens, displaying every image on the roll, as shown in Figure 2-7. If you have more than one roll of film, you can select and view any roll to see the individual digital pictures.

The images you see, often called *thumbnails,* are pretty small (otherwise they wouldn't all fit on one page). Click one of the images to see a larger version of the picture. As an alternative, you can select the check box alongside a picture and then click the View Full Picture button at the bottom of the Roll Viewer page.

While viewing the larger version of your picture on the resulting Full Picture page, notice the Next Picture and Previous Picture buttons along with a thumbnail preview of each. Click either button to move through your roll, displaying a larger-sized image of each photo as you go.

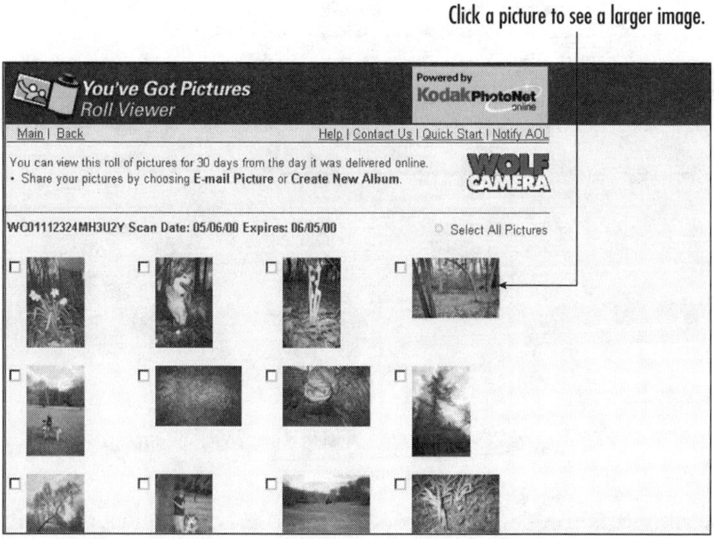

Figure 2-7. The Roll Viewer page displays every photo on your roll.

If you'd rather not step through the roll one shot after another, like a slide show, click the Back link at the top left of the Full Picture page. You skip right back to the Roll Viewer page, where you can select a different picture to view up close.

Renaming a Roll

After you have a good look at a roll, you will probably want to change its title from WC01112324MH3U2Y (or whatever random number the photo processor dishes out) to something more descriptive. If you're not already there, open the New Rolls page (see Figure 2-6), click a radio button to select the roll you want to rename, and click the Rename Roll button at the bottom of the New Rolls page. This opens the Rename Roll page.

The roll name that you choose can contain 20 characters, including letters, numbers, spaces, and common punctuation marks. The name change is only for your convenience.

"You've Got Pictures" — But Still Missing a Roll?

There's nothing worse than thinking your pictures have been lost, which is why "You've Got Pictures" has a button especially for people who can't find their pictures. On the New Rolls page, click the Don't See Your Roll button, which opens the Don't See Your Roll page, as shown in Figure 2-8.

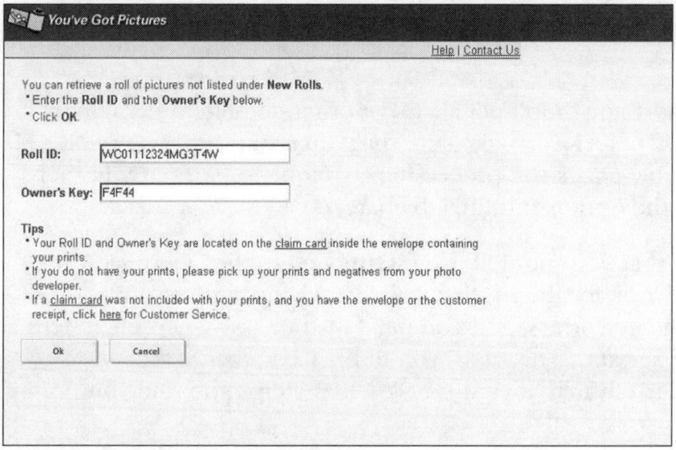
You've Got Pictures
Help | Contact Us
You can retrieve a roll of pictures not listed under New Rolls.
• Enter the Roll ID and the Owner's Key below.
• Click OK.
Roll ID: WC01112324MG3T4W
Owner's Key: F4F44
Tips
• Your Roll ID and Owner's Key are located on the claim card inside the envelope containing your prints.
• If you do not have your prints, please pick up your prints and negatives from your photo developer.
• If a claim card was not included with your prints, and you have the envelope or the customer receipt, click here for Customer Service.
Ok
Cancel

Figure 2-8. Retrieve missing rolls from this page.

Every roll of film scanned by "You've Got Pictures" gets a unique Roll ID and an Owner's Key, both of which are printed on a card that comes inside the envelope containing your prints. Type them into the appropriate boxes in the Don't See Your Roll page and click the OK button at the bottom of the page.

Your pictures may not have arrived in your New Rolls window for several reasons:

- You gave the photo lab a different screen name. Look at the card containing the Roll ID and Owner's Key, or look at the envelope from the photo lab. Either item should show the screen name that was used for "You've Got Pictures." Switch to the screen name you gave to the lab and see if your pictures are there.
- There was a typographical error in your screen name, or you misspelled your screen name. If you see a typo or misspelling, use the Roll ID and Owner's Key to retrieve your photos.
- The name or telephone number you gave to the photo lab doesn't match your AOL account information and screen name(s). This security measure prevents the wrong person from accidentally receiving your photos, but may also prevent you from accessing your photos. Go to AOL Keyword: **Billing**, click the Change Your Name or Address link, and type in your current information.

Note: Only Master screen names can change AOL Billing information.

What happens if you didn't get a card or other document containing a Roll ID and Owner's Key? Make sure that you requested "You've Got Pictures." Double-check the processing envelope to find out whether you checked the option and the lab charged you for that service.

If you're sure that you should have pictures, go to the Don't See Your Roll page and look for the tip that says, "If a claim card was not included with your prints, or if you need further assistance, click here for Customer Service." This takes you to the Customer Service Roll Assistance page (shown in Figure 2-9), which helps you find your missing pictures.

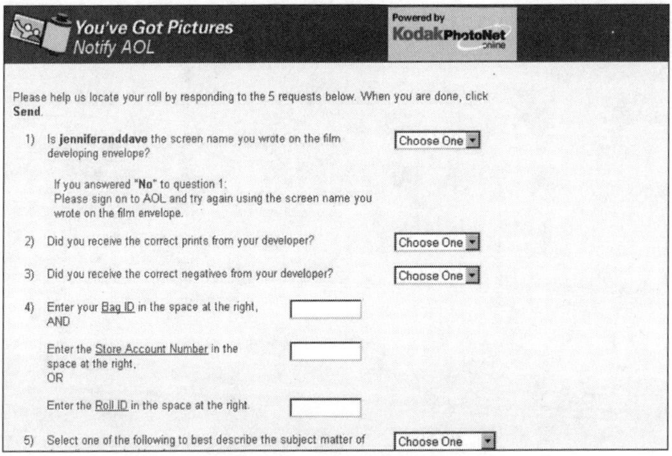

Figure 2-9. AOL helps you find your missing roll of pictures.

Viewing Your Uploaded Pictures

You don't need to buy any new equipment to use "You've Got Pictures"; you can enter a new world of sharing images and creating fun projects by using the film camera you already have. But by investing in equipment beyond your film camera, you can greatly expand your sources for digital pictures — and have fun in the process. Here are a couple of common types of equipment that can help you do more with online pictures:

- **A digital camera:** With a digital camera, you can take pictures just as with a traditional camera, but a major difference is that you can see your images right away. And as soon as you get back to your PC, you can transfer image files to your computer and upload them to "You've Got Pictures" for ordering photo-quality prints, storing, and sharing online.
- **A scanner:** With a scanner, you can convert any old photographic print into a digital image (whether it's 100 years old or 1 day old), upload it to "You've Got Pictures," store it, share it with others, and use it in other ways.

Chapter 4 tells you how to upload the pictures from equipment such as a digital camera or a scanner to the "You've Got Pictures" service. After you upload your pictures, they're available for viewing in the Saved Pictures tab of "You've Got Pictures" (refer to Figure 2-6).

Chapter 3

Sharing Your Pictures Through E-Mail

In This Chapter

- Sharing your pictures online
- Attaching pictures to e-mail
- E-mailing pictures from "You've Got Pictures"
- Embedding pictures in your e-mail messages

Whether you're a proud parent showing off your toddler's antics, or a shutterbug bursting to show your latest, greatest pictures to the world, sharing your pictures online is key. "You've Got Pictures" makes it easy to get your pictures online and then share them in a variety of ways. Sharing pictures through e-mail is a common and versatile way to pass around your photos. This chapter tells you how.

Ways to Share Your Pictures

"You've Got Pictures" and related AOL features add a whole new dimension to the act of sharing pictures online. Did you know that an e-mail message can carry more than a simple text message? It can hand-deliver your pictures, too.

E-mail is available throughout AOL: It's built into "You've Got Pictures," it's integral to the AOL service (note the AOL toolbar's Read and Write buttons), and it's even available on the Web at `www.aol.com/aolmail`.

Avenues for embedding, attaching, and sending your pictures through e-mail include the following:

- Sending your e-mail message directly from the "You've Got Pictures" service
- Embedding a picture in your message from the Write Mail window
- Sending your picture as an attachment to your e-mail message
- Using the AOL Picture Gallery as a source for pictures to embed in e-mail messages

Sending E-Mail from "You've Got Pictures"

Life doesn't get simpler than this. Go to "You've Got Pictures" (AOL Keyword: **Pictures**), select the picture you want to e-mail, supply the e-mail address and a brief message, and "You've Got Pictures" does the rest.

When your recipients belong to AOL, they receive a message with an *embedded* picture — the picture appears within the message itself — so they don't have to download the picture or even click a link.

If some of the recipients are not AOL members, they receive e-mail messages containing a *link* (Web address) and — depending on the e-mail application they are using — either an attached file or a picture embedded in the e-mail message. The recipients can choose to download the picture or click the link to visit the Buddy Picture Web page created for this purpose. Here's how you share a digital picture using "You've Got Pictures":

Note: These steps apply to Saved Pictures, New Rolls, My Albums, and Buddy Albums.

1. At AOL Keyword: **Pictures** ("You've Got Pictures"), view the picture(s) you want to send. You can send any picture that's in the New Roll, Saved Pictures, My Albums, or Buddy Albums tabs. For this example, click the Saved Pictures tab.

2. Find the picture you want to send and click the check box next to the picture, as shown in Figure 3-1.

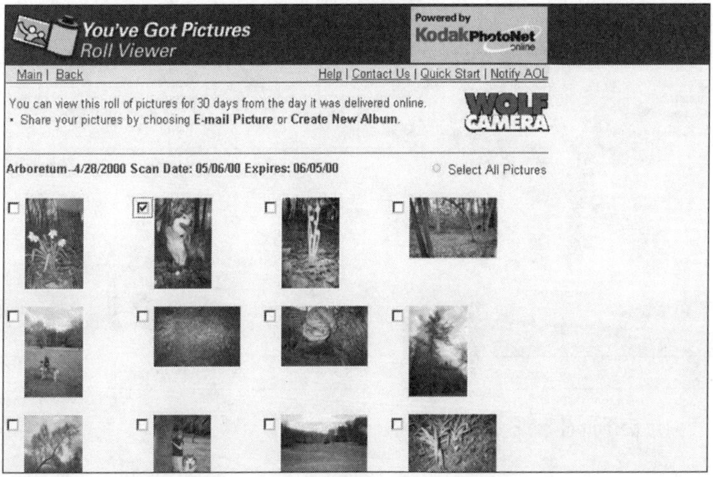

Figure 3-1. Select a saved picture by placing a check in the box next to it.

3. Click the E-Mail Picture button at the top or bottom of the Saved Pictures page to open the E-Mail a Picture page, shown in Figure 3-2.

4. Enter the addresses of any recipients. You can select an address two ways:
   - If you've previously sent digital pictures to the address, select that address from the Recent Recipients drop-down list. Select the Add All Names option to send the picture to every name on that list.
   - If an e-mail address isn't in the Recent Recipients list, just type it into the Send To box. Use the screen name of AOL members (for example, `JenniferAndDave`) or type the full Internet e-mail address of non-members (for example, `YGPuser@passporter.com`).

Tip If you'll be e-mailing photos to many of the people on the Recent Recipients list, select the Add All Names option and then delete any addresses you don't want to use in the Send To box.

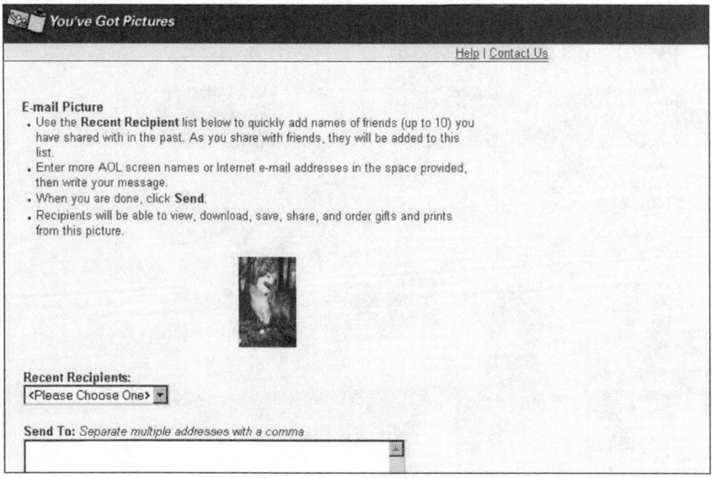
You've Got Pictures
Help | Contact Us
E-mail Picture
• Use the Recent Recipient list below to quickly add names of friends (up to 10) you have shared with in the past. As you share with friends, they will be added to this list.
• Enter more AOL screen names or Internet e-mail addresses in the space provided, then write your message.
• When you are done, click Send.
• Recipients will be able to view, download, save, share, and order gifts and prints from this picture.
Recent Recipients:
<Please Choose One>
Send To: Separate multiple addresses with a comma

Figure 3-2. The top portion of the E-Mail Picture page.

Tip: If you're sending the picture to several people, separate their addresses with a comma. The new names that you enter are automatically added to the Recent Recipients list for future use.

5. Type your message in the Message box.
6. When everything is set to go, click the Send button.

"You've Got Pictures"' e-mail does have its limitations:

- You can't format or change the font of your text.
- If you normally use a signature line in your e-mail, it won't appear in your "You've Got Pictures" mail.
- Further, each e-mail message can contain only one picture, so if you try to send more than one picture, "You've Got Pictures" tells you to send a Buddy Album instead. (Find out more about albums in Chapter 5.)
- A recipient receives your e-mail from a screen name called `AOL BuddyPics` (for an AOL member) or an e-mail address called `AOLYou'veGotPics@aol.com` (for an Internet address). The recipient can't easily reply to the message. If you'd prefer to have your own e-mail address displayed in the From line, compose your own e-mail as discussed in the next section.

Inserting Pictures into AOL E-Mail Messages

AOL members can compose an AOL e-mail message with digital pictures embedded right in the body of the message. Unlike the e-mail created by "You've Got Pictures," your regular AOL e-mail can contain more than one image, the message can conclude with a signature, and you have many creative options for making great-looking messages.

First, you must have the digital picture somewhere on your computer hard drive or on another drive accessible by your computer. If the picture you want is online at "You've Got Pictures," download it at E-Mail & Web Page quality (see Chapter 4 for details). To insert a picture into an AOL e-mail message, follow these steps:

1. Click the Write icon on the AOL toolbar to open a Write Mail window (shown in Figure 3-3).
2. Enter your e-mail message. It's a good idea to start writing your e-mail message before you insert the picture because it's easier to position your picture(s) when there is text in the message box.

Click this button to insert a picture.

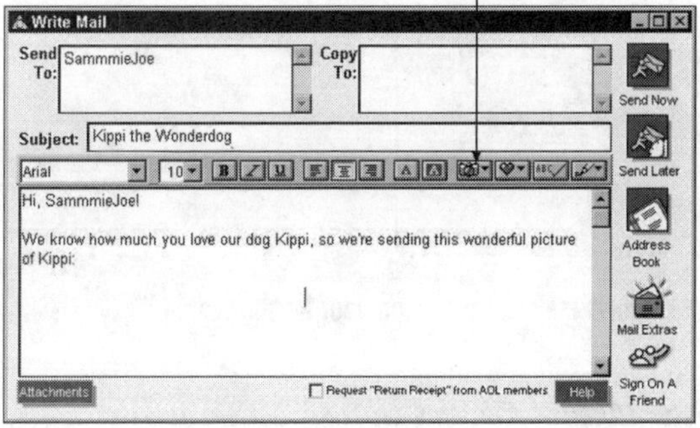

Figure 3-3. The AOL Write Mail window (Windows 95/98).

3. Click the Insert a Picture button on the Write Mail toolbar. And from the drop-down list that appears, select Insert a Picture.
4. In the Open dialog box, navigate to the folder containing your picture, select your picture, and click the Open button.

   Repeat Steps 3 and 4 to insert additional pictures, if you want.

After inserting a picture in an AOL e-mail message, you can use all the usual text-editing techniques, including copy, paste, cut, and delete. You can even highlight the image with your mouse and apply text formatting options to center the image on the page, or to align left or align right.

Using Picture Gallery to Insert Photos in E-Mail

Another tool for inserting pictures in an AOL e-mail message is the AOL Picture Gallery, which displays every picture in a single folder on your hard drive, as shown in Figure 3-4. With the Picture Gallery open, you can drag a picture into an open Write Mail window (click the picture, move it, and release the mouse button).

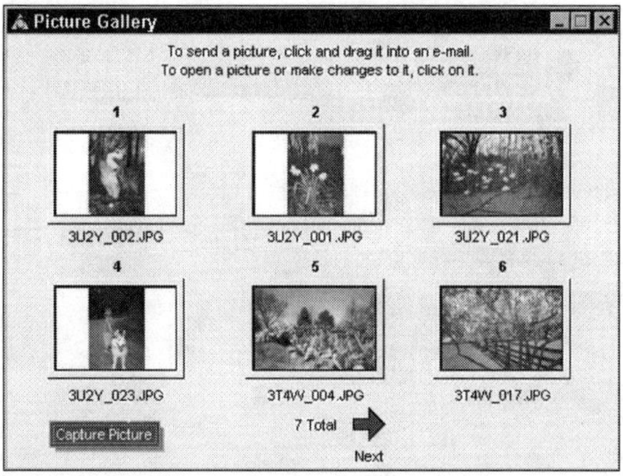

Figure 3-4. The AOL Picture Gallery displays the picture files on your hard drive.

Follow these steps to use the Picture Gallery to insert a photo in an e-mail message:

1. To open the Picture Gallery, choose File⇨Open Picture Gallery from the menu bar.
2. In the Open Picture Gallery dialog box, select the folder containing the pictures you want to view and click Open Gallery.
3. Single-click a displayed picture to open it in AOL's built-in image Picture Gallery editor, which you can use to rotate, crop, and resize the photo as well as adjust the contrast and brightness.

4. When you're done editing the image, you can save the result and then drag the picture into a message in a Write Mail window. Or you can just click the handy Insert in Email button in the image editor window.

Tip: AOL Mail Extras is a collection of pictures, clip art, effects, and other digital images that you can insert to jazz up your AOL e-mail. Just click the Mail Extras button in any Write Mail window.

Attaching Digital Pictures to AOL Mail

Yet another way to share photos via e-mail is to *attach* them to an e-mail message. An attached file is not part of the message itself, but the recipient can download the file if he or she wants to see it. AOL e-mail allows you to *attach* one or more files of any kind to an e-mail. Attaching photos makes sense in the following situations:

- You're sending e-mail to Internet recipients. Because they can't view *inserted* pictures, you must *attach* pictures that you want to share with them.
- You're sending several photos and want to compress the size of the photos for quicker transfer.
- You know that your recipient intends to download the picture but has no need to view it at the same time he or she reads the message.

Note: Because many members are cautious about opening messages with embedded pictures or attachments, you may want to consider creating a Buddy Album as a safe alternative and informing your recipients in the subject line that you're sending digital pictures.

To attach one or more photos to an AOL e-mail, follow these steps:

1. Download the photos that you want to send from "You've Got Pictures" or from your scanner or digital camera. Chapter 4 has more information about downloading images.
2. Open the AOL software and click the Write icon on the toolbar. A new, blank Write Mail window opens for you.
3. Fill in the recipient's screen name or e-mail address, a descriptive subject line, and a message explaining the photo(s) you're sending.

4. Click the Attachments button in the lower left-hand corner of the Write Mail window. The Attachments window appears, as shown in Figure 3-5.

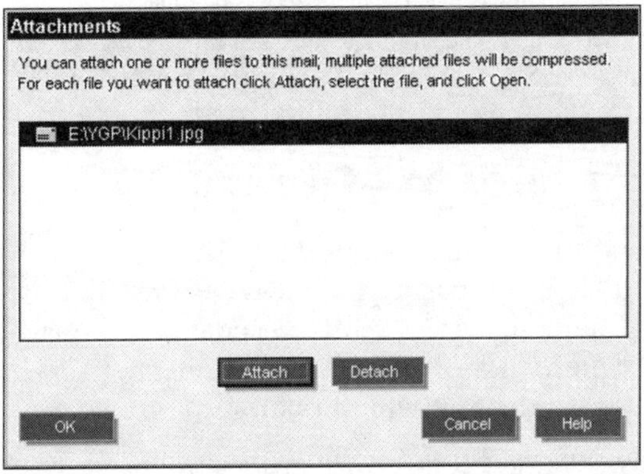
Attachments
You can attach one or more files to this mail; multiple attached files will be compressed.
For each file you want to attach click Attach, select the file, and click Open.
E:\YGP\Kippi1.jpg
Attach
Detach
OK
Cancel
Help

Figure 3-5. The Attachments window lists files you're attaching.

5. Click the Attach button in the Attachments window.
6. In the Attach dialog box that appears, find and select the first photo file you want to attach and then click Open. The dialog box disappears, and your first photo file is listed in the Attachments window (refer to Figure 3-5).
7. Repeat Steps 5 and 6 to add more files, if you want.
8. After you've selected the last picture, click OK in the Attachments window. Your Write Mail window now shows the name of the *first* file that you attached next to the Attachments button, along with a new icon (two floppy disks). You can review your attached files by clicking the Attachments button again.
9. When you're ready to send the message, click the Send Now button to send your e-mail and any attached file. If you attached more than one file, AOL compresses the files.

Whether your e-mail recipients are AOL members or non-members, their mailboxes indicate that the message has an attachment by displaying an icon — usually some variation of an envelope with a floppy disk attached to it.

Tip

The File Transfer dialog box appears every time you send or receive a file attachment via e-mail. If you're sending a large file or a set of files or have completed your online business for the day, you may want to select the Sign Off After Transfer check box in the progress dialog box. Selecting this option means that AOL will sign off when it's finished sending the file(s). Alternatively, you can click the Send Later button and use Auto AOL to send your e-mail at another time. Choose Mail Center⇨Set Up Automatic AOL from the toolbar to configure Auto AOL.

Downloading Pictures Attached to E-Mail

How do your recipients download a picture attached to an e-mail message? AOL members who have *not* blocked attached files at AOL Keyword: **Mail Controls** receive the e-mail in their mailboxes as usual.

Caution

Never download attached files from individuals you do not know or from anyone claiming to be an AOL employee or "You've Got Pictures" employee (neither will e-mail attached files to an AOL member).

Here's how to download an attachment if you're an AOL member:

1. Open the e-mail that contains the attached file.
2. Click the Download Now button in the lower-left corner of the e-mail. If an E-Mail Attachment Warning appears, read it carefully and click Yes if you want to continue.
3. Select a good location for the file on your computer and click the Save button.

   AOL displays a progress thermometer as the file downloads. If the estimated download time is longer than you want to wait, you can click Finish Later. Keep in mind, however, that you can do many other things while the file downloads.
4. If the attached file is a common graphic file (and contains a single picture instead of several zipped pictures), AOL displays the image as it downloads.

If the file you downloaded was compressed (for example, the filename ends in `.ZIP` or `.SIT`), you need to decompress the file before you can view it. You can do this using AOL's Download Manager. To decompress a file you've already downloaded using AOL, follow these steps:

1. Choose My Files⇨Download Manager from the toolbar. Click Show Files Downloaded to see a list of downloaded files, as shown in Figure 3-6.

Definition

Compressing files is an efficient way of sending a few of them at once — rather than sending several e-mail messages, each with one file. When you decompress the file, individual items are *extracted*, or pulled out.

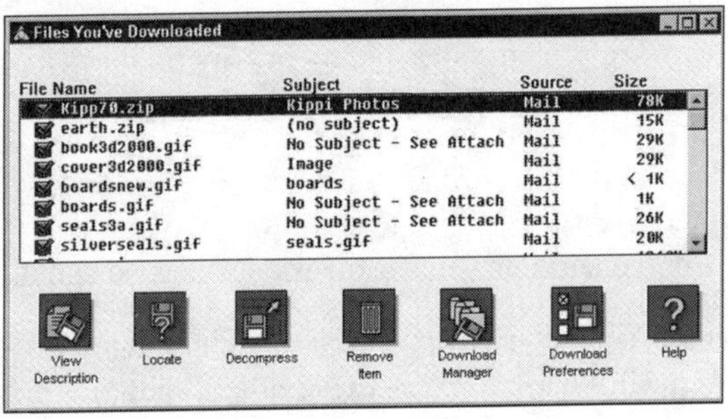

Figure 3-6. A handy-dandy list of downloaded files.

2. After you locate and select the file you want to decompress, click it with your mouse and then click the Decompress button. A window appears, showing the progress of the decompression.

   When the decompression is complete, you see a File Transfer Status window, which shows the number of items extracted from the file. To locate downloaded files, click Show Files Downloaded, select the file just unzipped, and click Locate.

3. Choose File⇨Open from the menu bar, find the files you just downloaded, and open them. Most image files will open and display in AOL, including files you've downloaded from "You've Got Pictures."

Parental Controls and Safe Sharing

Not everyone can view e-mail containing embedded pictures of the kind sent by You've Got Mail. AOL provides Parental Controls (AOL Keyword: **Parental Controls**) so that parents can protect their young ones (and themselves) from viewing pictures from strangers.

These controls allow parents to set their minors' screen names to one of several age categories. Children whose screen names are set to Kids Only or Young Teens cannot receive e-mail containing pictures or attached files.

Parental Controls also includes a Custom Controls feature so that e-mail with pictures or attached files can be blocked from any screen name, not just screen names set to Young Teens or Kids Only. Parental Controls are available from many places on AOL, for example, through a button on the Welcome Screen and from AOL Keyword: **Parental Controls**. The main Parental Controls screen is shown in Figure 3-7.

When adult AOL members receive e-mail with pictures or attached files, AOL posts a warning message to inform them of the possible dangers of pictures or files sent by strangers. If you do not receive such a warning, it means that at some point you chose to not receive it. You can reinstate the warning, though. Choose My AOL⇨Preferences⇨Graphics from the AOL toolbar and select the Notify before Opening Mail Containing Pictures check box.

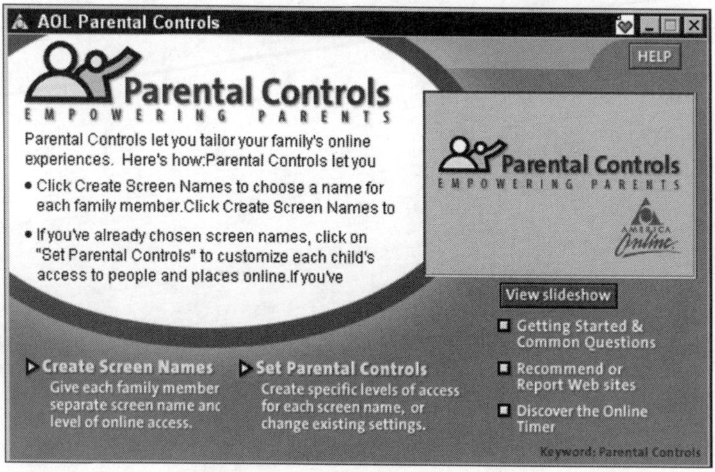

Figure 3-7. The main Parental Controls screen leads you to many sources of information about child safety and to AOL's tools for keeping kids safe.

Chapter 4

Gathering and Organizing Your Pictures

In This Chapter

- Saving your pictures on "You've Got Pictures"
- Downloading pictures to your computer
- Uploading pictures to "You've Got Pictures"
- Renaming and tracking your online pictures

AOL offers a complete range of resources to assist in all your activities with digital pictures. "You've Got Pictures" (AOL Keyword: **Pictures**) makes it as easy as possible for AOL members to get digital pictures by providing an easy-to-use online service for collecting, managing, using, and sharing digital pictures. Whether you're looking for storage space or help with downloading or uploading pictures, AOL and "You've Got Pictures" can assist.

Managing Your Pictures Online

After you successfully receive your online photos at "You've Got Pictures," the clock begins to tick. You have 30 days to save your new roll(s) to your storage space. After 30 days, the pictures that you've chosen to save remain online until you delete them yourself; all unsaved digital pictures are deleted.

You have to decide whether you want to save some or all of those pictures, or let them disappear from your account. Or you can download the pictures to your PC and store them on your hard drive.

Saving Individual Pictures

When all the pictures in a roll are displayed in the Roll Viewer (shown in Figure 4-1), you can save one or more pictures by selecting the check box next to any picture and then clicking the Save button at the bottom of the page. Or, select the Select All Pictures radio button before clicking Save.

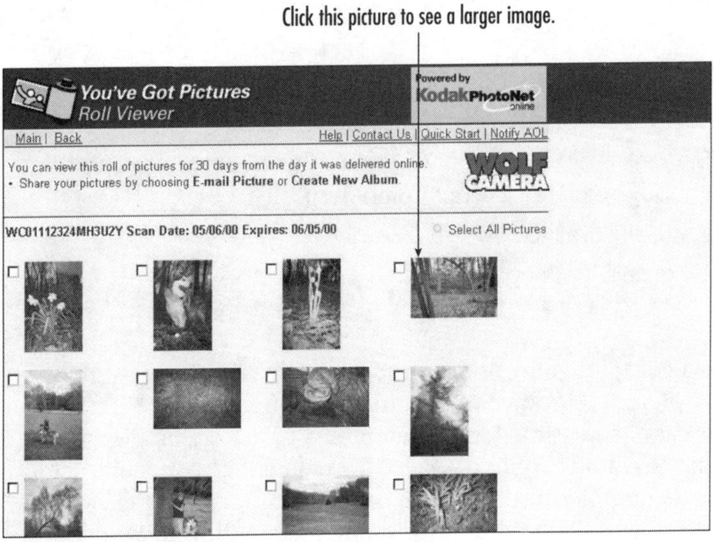

Figure 4-1. The Roll Viewer page displays every photo on your roll.

Your digital pictures are saved (stored) online. You get 30 days free rent with every roll you process, and *every screen name* on your account has permanent, unlimited free storage space as long as you are an AOL member and visit the "You've Got Pictures" area at least once in a 6-month period. If you discontinue your AOL service or you don't visit "You've Got Pictures" within 6 months, your saved pictures will be deleted.

Tip To save your pictures before they expire, store them online on your Saved Pictures tab. AOL provides its current members with unlimited free storage space provided that they remain AOL members and visit "You've Got Pictures" once in a 6-month period. Once they are stored online, your pictures don't expire unless you delete them. You can also download them to your hard drive or to a floppy disk.

Saving Entire Rolls

You can save an entire roll with a few clicks of your mouse. Just follow these steps:

1. Click the New Rolls tab in "You've Got Pictures".
2. Select the roll that you want to save by clicking Select (adjacent to that roll).
3. Click the Save Roll button toward the bottom of that screen. A new window appears, asking whether you're sure you want to save the roll.
4. Click OK or Cancel, depending on your needs.

After your roll has been saved, you find all the pictures on the Saved Pictures tab.

Downloading Pictures to Your Computer

If "You've Got Pictures" is such a useful way to collect your digital pictures, why would you want to download them to your own computer? Here are a few reasons:

- To edit them with image-editing software such as MGI PhotoSuite.
- To use your digital pictures in Web pages (see Chapter 6).
- To use your digital pictures in photo activities for work or home, including greeting cards, family trees, newsletters, and invitations.

Downloading without Pain

When you download files of any type, you copy them to your computer. In doing this, you are *not* removing them from the source from which they are downloaded. "You've Got Pictures" lets you download one or several pictures at a time; you can even download an entire roll. Follow these steps to download digital pictures:

1. Go to AOL Keyword: **Pictures**.
2. If you have previously saved the pictures, click the Saved Pictures tab.

If the pictures are part of a new roll, click the New Roll tab, select the roll you want to view, and click the View button. From there, you can see a set of small pictures from which to select.

3. Find the picture you want to download and select the check box next to it. You can download more than one picture at a time by selecting more than one check box. Or you can click the Select All Pictures radio button in the upper-right corner of the window to select all the pictures.
4. Click the Download Pictures button at the bottom of the page.
5. On the next page (shown in Figure 4-2), select one of these resolutions:

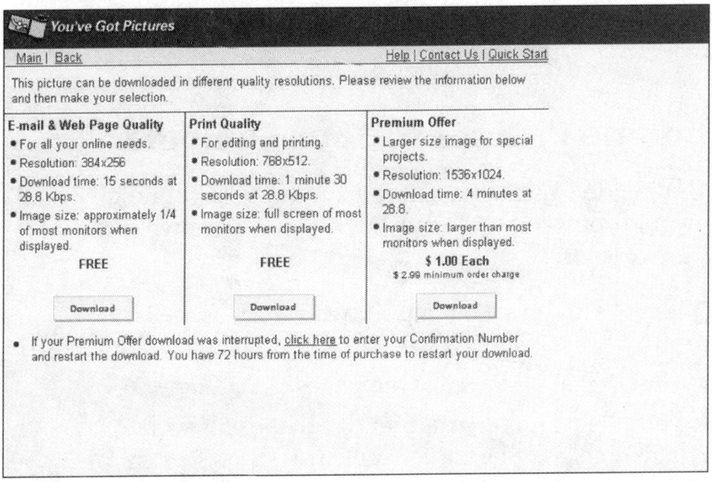

Figure 4-2. When downloading a picture, choose the resolution that suits your needs.

- **E-mail & Web Page Quality:** Select this resolution if you'll be using your digital picture as an e-mail attachment or on a Web page.
- **Print Quality:** Select this resolution if you want to print the picture or edit it with graphics software.
- **Premium Offer:** This is the highest resolution, appropriate for those important pictures and special projects. See the Premium Offer information on the page for more info about this option.

Note Keep in mind that with high resolutions, the picture is larger, the download time is longer, and the print quality is better.

6. If you selected the Premium Quality resolution, you can skip the remainder of these steps. If you selected the E-mail and Web Page Quality option or the Print Quality option, click the Download Pictures button in the page that appears.
7. In the File Download dialog box, shown in Figure 4-3, make sure that the Save This Program to Disk radio button is selected and then click OK.

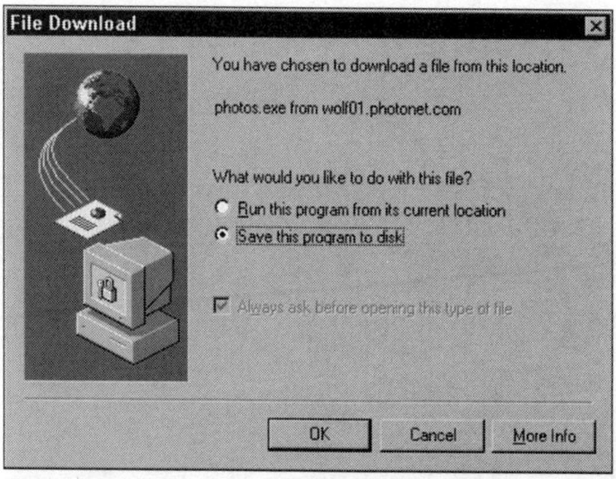

Figure 4-3. You see this dialog box when you begin the downloading process.

8. In the Save As dialog box, indicate where you want the pictures to be saved.

   While the picture downloads, the Windows Download dialog box tracks its progress. When the download is done, the dialog box reads Download Complete. Do *not* put a check in the Close This Dialog Box When Download Completes check box.

Before you can view the pictures you downloaded, you need to extract the pictures from the file you just downloaded by following these steps:

1. Click the Open Folder button in the Download Complete dialog box. You now see the contents of the America Online 5.0/Download folder (or the folder in which you chose to save your downloaded pictures), with the just-downloaded file, `photos.exe`, highlighted.
2. Double-click the downloaded file. The progress of "extracting" your pictures from `photos.exe` is shown in a small text window with a black background. During the process, the file or files containing your digital picture(s) are listed. The names of the picture files have weird numbers, so you might want to make a note of these numbers. For each picture being extracted, you'll see a line that reads

   ```
   Inflating: /.X67N_001.jpg
   Inflating: /.X67N_002.jpg
   etc.
   ```

   In place of `X67N_001.jpg` and `X67N_002.jpg`, and so on, you'll see the names of the files with *your* pictures.
3. Your digital pictures can now be viewed! Scroll through the Download folder to find your file and double click. See Figure 4-4.

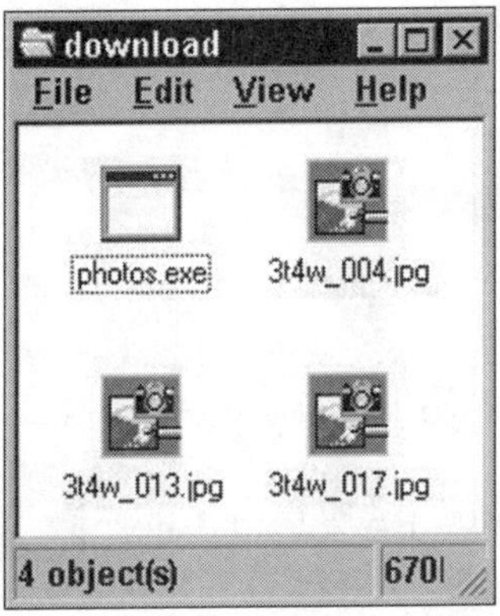

Figure 4-4. A folder with digital pictures, ready to be viewed.

4. Double-click the file to view it. A default image-viewing application such as Windows Paint Shop Pro then opens. Or, from AOL, select the file using File⇨Open or File⇨Open Picture Gallery.

Renaming and Copying Your Downloaded Pictures

To view your pictures, choose File⇨Open Picture Gallery from the AOL toolbar. Navigate to the folder that contains the downloaded pictures and click the Open Gallery button to see your images.

The first thing you'll notice about a downloaded digital picture is the weird file name, something ugly like `ZHUW_007.jpg`, or worse. Such numbers are useless because they have no relationship to the content of your picture.

To rename a picture you've just downloaded, follow these steps:

1. **Find the folder that contains the file you want to rename (which is probably the Download folder) and then right-click the file you want to rename.**
2. **Choose Rename from the context menu that appears.**
3. **Type in a new filename for the picture but don't change the file type (the `.JPG` part).** You may want to rename your files with AOL Picture Gallery open, so you can quickly match the filename to what's in the actual picture.

Next, you need to copy your pictures to the folder in which you'll be storing and using them. To copy picture files from the folder into which they were download to another folder:

1. **Open Windows Explorer and display the folder into which you want to copy the downloaded pictures.**
2. **Double-click the Download folder or whatever folder you used to download from "You've Got Pictures."**
3. **For a single picture, just click it once to select it. For more than one picture, hold down the Ctrl key and click each picture you want to copy. For many pictures in a row, hold Shift and click the first and last pictures in the sequence. When you're done, right-click and choose Copy.**

Tip: Choose Cut instead of Copy if you want to remove the file from the folder into which it was downloaded and avoid cluttering up your hard drive.

4. **Switch to the folder you selected in Step 1. Then right-click the folder and choose Paste.** Your pictures are then copied into the folder.

Uploading Pictures to "You've Got Pictures"

From time to time, you may want to *upload* digital pictures to "You've Got Pictures" in order to store them online, order prints or photo gifts, and share them with others by e-mail or as part of an online album. (Uploading means *copying* a file from your computer to an Internet-connected computer.) Uploading stores your images online at "You've Got Pictures," along with your other saved pictures. Anything you can do with pictures processed by a participating developer and stored on "You've Got Pictures" can be done with any pictures you upload from your computer. You can

- Share them with others using the "You've Got Pictures" e-mail and Buddy Albums (see Chapters 3 and 5)
- Order photographic quality prints (see Chapter 7)
- Use them in products such as coffee mugs and the like (see Chapter 7)

Getting Digital Pictures from a Camera

Before you can upload digital pictures (that come from your camera) to "You've Got Pictures," you have to first get them from the camera to your computer. The process for transferring digital pictures, called *downloading*, is not hard, but giving generalized download instructions can be a bit difficult. The specific transfer process varies by digital camera and editing software, and many cameras offer a choice of downloading methods. For example, the AOL PhotoCam lets you download your pictures from the camera to your computer by using a cable that links the two (camera and computer, that is).

You can transfer pictures from a digital camera to your PC in three different ways. The following bullet list briefly describes these transfer methods:

- **Capture pictures directly onto a floppy (3½-inch) disk.** When the disk is full, remove the disk from the camera and place it in your PC's floppy drive, where you can transfer the images directly to your PC. Currently, the Sony Mavica is one of the few digital cameras offering built-in floppy support.
- **Let your PC read the camera's memory card directly.** Some memory cards can be placed in a special adapter and inserted into either the A drive or an inexpensive reading

device. The beauty of removable cards is that you can remove them and buy larger amounts of additional memory.

- **Use a serial cable (cord).** Most cameras use a serial cable (cord) attached to the camera on one end and connected to a PC's serial port (usually on the back of a PC) on the other end. More and more cameras come with Universal Serial Bus (USB) cables that can be plugged into a newer kind of port (also called *Universal Serial Bus*) on the computer. USB connections are becoming standard issue on new PCs.

Getting Digital Pictures from a Scanner

Using a scanner provides another source for digital pictures that you can upload from your computer to "You've Got Pictures." A scanner works much like a photocopy machine, but the result of scanning something is an electronic file rather than a piece of paper. When you scan a photographic print, you wind up with a file containing a digital picture.

What do you need in order to scan? Of course, you must have a scanner attached to your computer, and you need the software that comes with your scanner installed on your computer. You can then log on to AOL and follow these basic steps to scan a photo.

1. Choose Edit⇨Capture Picture from the AOL menu bar to bring up the Capture Picture window, as shown in Figure 4-5.

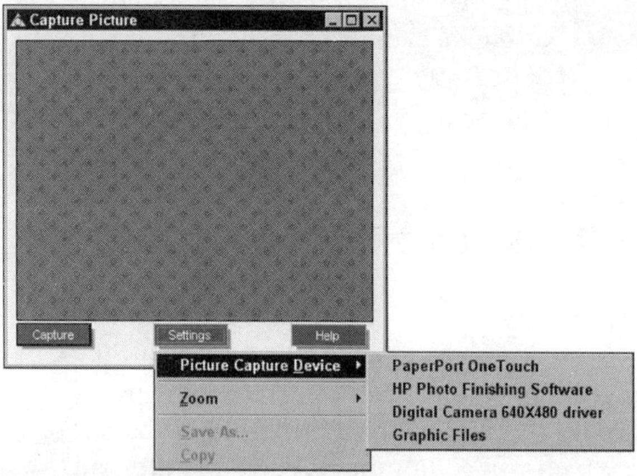

Figure 4-5. The Capture Picture window.

2. Choose Settings⇨Picture Capture Device and select the scanner software you want to use to create the scanned image. AOL provides a menu of likely programs, making your job easier.
3. Position the image you want to scan (such as a photographic print) on your scanner; then click the Capture button in the Capture Picture window.

   Your scanner software's window probably lets you specify how you want to do the scan — in black and white or color, with high or less-high quality, with greater or lesser contrast, at a certain size, and so on.
4. To begin the scan, follow the instructions provided by your scanning software.

   You'll know that the scan is done when the scanner stops and the software's progress indicators indicate that the job has been completed.
5. After the scanner is finished scanning, complete the process by saving the scanned file with a specific name, file type, and folder location.

   "You've Got Pictures" accepts several file types, including JPG, GIF, and BMP. Unless you have a specific need, save the scanned image as a JPG file, the most common type of graphic file used on the World Wide Web.

Following the Easy Uploading Instructions

You may already have digital pictures on your hard drive. Whether those pictures came from your digital camera or from photos that you scanned, you can upload them to "You've Got Pictures." Look for the Upload Picture button on both the Saved Pictures and My Albums tabs.

Here's how the uploading process works:

1. Go to AOL Keyword: **Pictures**.
   - To upload a picture, click the Saved Pictures tab and then click Upload Picture.
   - To upload a digital picture to a specific album (a collection of digital pictures you can maintain at "You've Got Pictures"), click the My Albums tab, select the radio button to the left of the album into which you want to import the picture, and click Upload Picture. Albums are discussed in Chapter 5.

2. Follow the instructions on the on-screen page: Preview the picture before uploading it and then click Upload Picture to upload it.

Note: You can upload only one picture at a time to "You've Got Pictures," but you can download several at a time.

"You've Got Pictures" can accept uploaded pictures in several popular graphics file formats, including JPG (or JPEG), GIF, and BMP. "You've Got Pictures" recommends that your images have a resolution of at least 640 x 480 if you intend to order picture merchandise with those images. See Chapter 7 for more information on "You've Got Pictures" merchandise.

Deleting Pictures from "You've Got Pictures"

With frequent use of the "You've Got Pictures" service, it's easy to find that you have several rolls of pictures online and several albums (on the My Albums or Buddy Albums tabs) that you've sent or received. Because "You've Got Pictures" offers unlimited free storage space, this isn't really a bad thing. However, you may decide that you'd like to delete a few individual pictures or entire albums from your online storage.

"You've Got Pictures" makes it easy to delete the pictures that you no longer want to have available to download, share, or view online. The following sets of instructions tell you how to do it.

To delete saved pictures:

1. Go to AOL Keyword: **Pictures**.
2. From the resulting My Pictures page, click the Saved Pictures tab. Thumbnail versions of your saved pictures come into view along with a set of buttons along the top and bottom of the tab.
3. Click the check box so that a check mark appears next to the picture or pictures that you want to delete.
4. Click the Delete button at the top or bottom of the Saved Pictures tab. "You've Got Pictures" then shows you a confirmation screen with the picture(s) that you marked for deletion.
5. After verifying that these are the pictures you want to delete, click OK on the confirmation screen, and your pictures are deleted. If you change your mind, click the Cancel button, and your pictures remain in your saved pictures area.

To delete albums:

1. Go to AOL Keyword: **Pictures**.
2. From the resulting My Pictures page, click the My Albums tab. You'll see a list of the albums that you have created online.
3. Select the album that you want to delete by clicking the option button next to the album name. You can select only one album at a time.
4. Click the Delete button on the My Albums tab. "You've Got Pictures" then shows you a confirmation screen with the name of the album that you marked for deletion.
5. After verifying that you want to delete the named album, click OK on the confirmation screen, and your album is deleted. If you change your mind, click the Cancel button, and your album stays on the My Albums tab.

Chapter 5

Creating and Sharing Albums

In This Chapter

- Collecting pictures online
- Creating an album with "You've Got Pictures"
- Viewing your album online
- Sharing and receiving albums through e-mail
- Finding other places to share albums

Picture this: Your child is just learning to walk, and you've been snap-happy, taking plenty of digital pictures of her first steps. Naturally, you want to share your photos with friends and family members. You could print them out on that new inkjet printer and give away copies, or even e-mail your favorite shots to family and friends.

But prints and e-mailed photos may take more time and money than you're willing to invest. As this chapter describes, "You've Got Pictures" gives you a better way to share a collection of photos with others: Put them in online *albums* and send them to anyone who has Internet access!

Sharing Collections of Pictures (Albums)

Albums are a fun, easy way to organize your favorite photos and share them with others. Online albums can consist of up to 100 photos, which can be gathered from

- Your saved pictures in "You've Got Pictures"
- Your Buddy Albums (that is, albums that others have shared with you)
- Pictures uploaded from your own computer

After you've chosen the photos for your album, you can personalize the album presentation with background colors, titles, and captions. When your album is ready, you can share it online with people that you specify.

Creating and Viewing Albums

If you want to make an album composed of many pictures from the same roll of film, the easiest way to create a new album is to visit AOL Keyword: **Pictures** and view a roll of pictures. If you want to create an album made of your favorite pictures from several rolls, begin in the Saved Pictures area.

Tip If you don't have any rolls, saved pictures, or Buddy Albums, you should consider uploading a picture. To do this, click the My Albums tab, click the Upload Picture button, and follow the directions for uploading, as explained in Chapter 4.

While viewing photos in either the New Rolls or Saved Pictures tab, follow these steps to make an album:

1. Select the photos you want to display in the album by selecting the check box to the left of each photo, as shown in Figure 5-1.

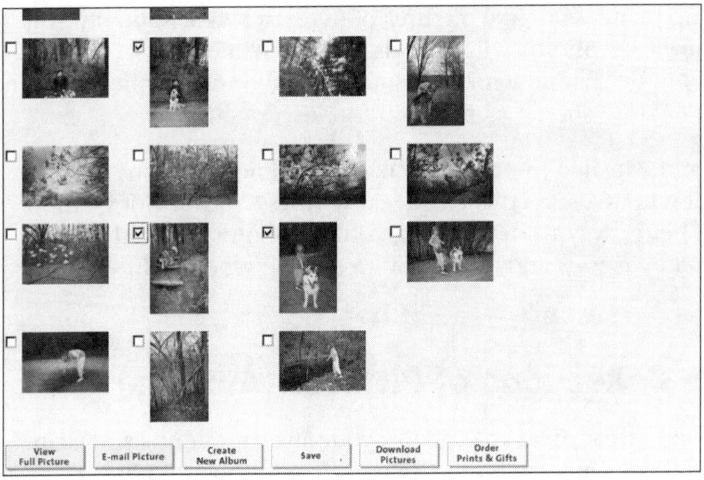

Figure 5-1. Select the photos for your new album.

2. Click the Create New Album button at the bottom of the window. "You've Got Pictures" displays the photos you selected for your new album, along with a default title (your screen name and the current date).
3. From here, you have three choices:
   - Customize your album (to make it more attractive for others)
   - Save your album (to stop for now or to keep the album as is)
   - Cancel

   For now, click the Save button — you can return to customize it later.
4. Next, you're prompted to agree to the "You've Got Pictures" terms — once you do, your new album is created.

You can take a look at your new album by clicking the View button. The "You've Got Pictures" Album Viewer (shown in Figure 5-2) displays your default title at the top, followed by your pictures, and gives you an array of options along the bottom.

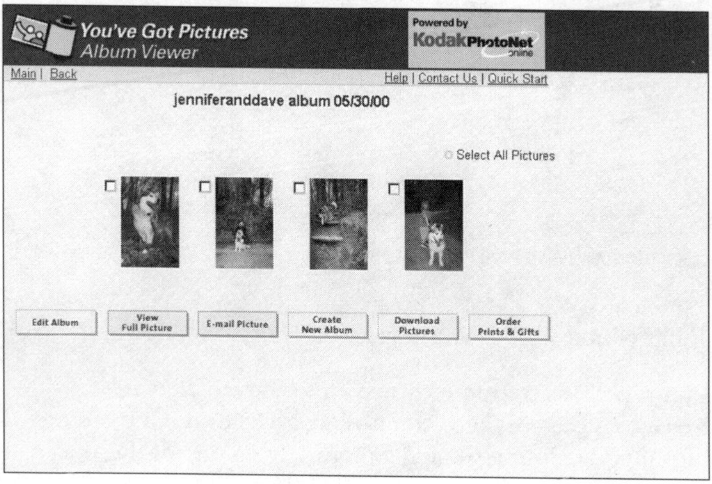

Figure 5-2. A new album, fresh from the computer.

Customizing and Editing an Album

After you create an album, you can customize it with a title, captions, a specific layout, and even a matching background. To begin customization, go to AOL Keyword: **Pictures**. Click the My Albums tab, select the album you want to customize, and click Edit to open the Edit Album window (see Figure 5-3).

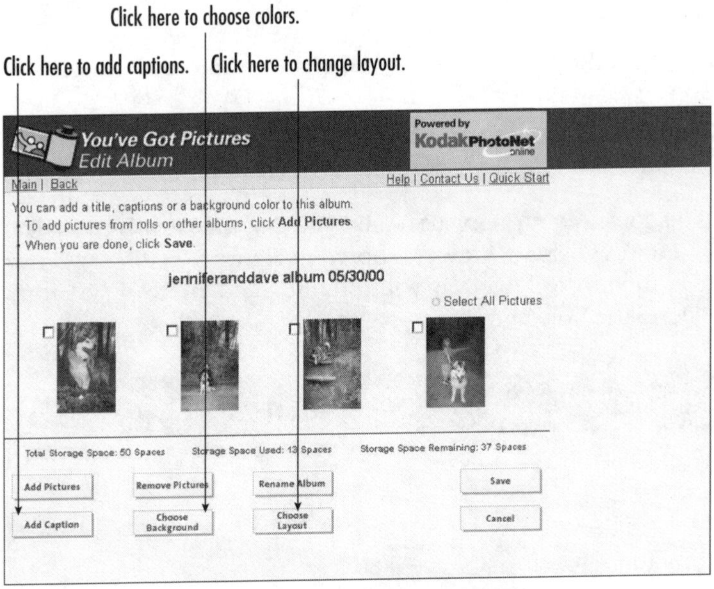

Figure 5-3. Customize your album from the Edit Album window.

The Edit Album window gives you several customization options:

- **Add Pictures.** This button returns you to the tab view of "You've Got Pictures" where you can access your rolls, saved pictures, and Buddy Albums. To add a picture from one of these sources, click the appropriate tab, select the photo(s) you want to add to your album, and click OK.

Tip

If you want the pictures in your album to display in a particular order, add each picture individually in the order you prefer. Each new picture is added to the end of the list of photos in your album.

- **Remove Pictures.** Click the check box next to the album pictures that you want to remove, click the Remove Pictures button, and confirm the removal. Don't worry; removing pictures from an album does *not* remove them from "You've Got Pictures."
- **Rename Album.** Click this button to type in a new name of up to 32 characters, plus a description of up to 60 characters, and then click OK. Be sure to include adequate identification for your album, like the date or season and a meaningful description.
- **Add Caption.** If you want to add captions to any photos, click the Add Caption button. The first photo in your album appears, along with space in which to type a caption of up to 32 characters. You can then click the Previous Pictures and Next Pictures buttons to add captions to other album photos. If you prefer to add a caption to a specific picture, select it in the album before clicking Add Caption.
- **Choose Background.** Click this button to choose from different-colored backgrounds. Select a color you like and click OK. At the time of writing, ten different colors are available. Avoid black and red, because they can make it very difficult to read the captions.
- **Choose Layout.** Clicking this button lets you choose how many photos are displayed per line: one, two, or four (default). Choose one for the largest possible picture display, two for medium sized pictures, and four for the smallest pictures. Click OK to save your changes.

Caution: Click the Save button to save your album customizations. If you sign off before you're able to save any changes, your modifications will be lost. To prevent this from happening, save your changes frequently.

Sharing an Album

Now that you've got a snazzy album filled with your favorite photos, show it off! To share an album, click the My Albums tab, select the album you want to share, and click Share. A new page appears, where you can indicate who should receive your album (see Figure 5-4).

Caution: All pictures that you share via AOL are subject to AOL's Terms of Service (TOS). It's a good idea to look over the rules regarding shared pictures at AOL Keyword: **TOS** and to read the "You've Got Pictures" Guidelines in the "You've Got Pictures" Help area.

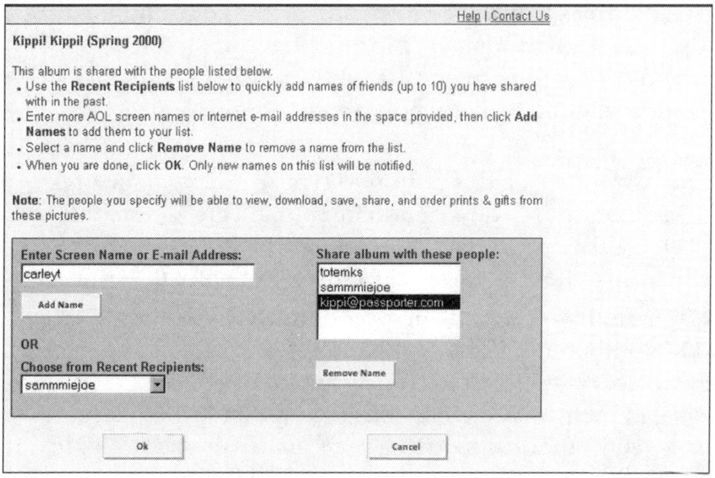
Help | Contact Us
Kippi! Kippi! (Spring 2000)
This album is shared with the people listed below.
• Use the Recent Recipients list below to quickly add names of friends (up to 10) you have shared with in the past.
• Enter more AOL screen names or Internet e-mail addresses in the space provided, then click Add Names to add them to your list.
• Select a name and click Remove Name to remove a name from the list.
• When you are done, click OK. Only new names on this list will be notified.
Note: The people you specify will be able to view, download, save, share, and order prints & gifts from these pictures.
Enter Screen Name or E-mail Address:
carleyt
Add Name
OR
Choose from Recent Recipients:
sammmiejoe
Share album with these people:
totemks
sammmiejoe
kippi@passporter.com
Remove Name
Ok
Cancel

Figure 5-4. Type the screen name or e-mail address of each person who should receive your album.

To add a name to the list of folks who can access your album, type each individual's exact e-mail address in the top field and click the Add Name button. If your recipient is an AOL member, you do not need to type the `@aol.com` after that person's screen name. All other e-mail addresses do require the @ symbol and domain name, however.

Tip You can share as many albums as you want, and each album can be shared with as many as 100 people. If you want to share an album with more than 100 people, simply create an identical album and begin a new list of screen names.

Each time you click the Add Name button, the page updates, and the recipient's e-mail address is added to the list on the right. Continue typing e-mail addresses and clicking Add Name until all recipients appear in the list. If you need to remove a recipient at any time, select that person's name in the list and click Remove Name.

Tip If you've shared albums before, the names of past recipients may appear in the Choose from Recent Recipients drop-down list. Select a name from this menu to add that person's name to your list.

After your list is complete, click the OK button to save your list and share your album. "You've Got Pictures" sends an e-mail to each recipient on your list announcing the availability of the new album. The message comes from the screen name `AOL BuddyPics` (if the recipients are AOL members) or `AOLYou'veGotPics@aol.com` (if they are not AOL members).

Note: You can share your favorite pictures or albums with anyone who uses e-mail, even non-AOL members. Non-members receive an e-mail instructing them to go to `pictures.aol.com` and enter their username and password, which are included in the e-mail. After viewing the pictures, non-members can save and download the pictures as well as order picture gifts and prints.

The message contains directions on how to access the shared album. For AOL recipients, the shared album now appears in their list of Buddy Albums (albums shared by someone else) at AOL Keyword: **Pictures**.

Receiving Buddy Albums

When someone sends *you* an album, you receive an e-mail from `AOL BuddyPics`. The "You've Got Pictures" icon on the Welcome Screen and voice alert will also tell you that you have new pictures.

To access an album that someone has shared with you, go to AOL Keyword: **Pictures**, click the Buddy Albums tab, select the new album, and click the View button. Shared albums offer many familiar options: view full picture, e-mail picture, create new album, download pictures, and order prints and gifts.

A new option is to save the Buddy Album, which stores the photos in your own storage space. Save a Buddy Album only if you really want *all* the pictures in the album saved in your saved pictures area. If you don't save the album, the photos remain accessible as long as the person who shared the album with you retains them. If you really like a particular photo, you may want to go ahead and save it in your own storage space.

Managing Albums

If you enjoy the albums feature, it's a good idea to learn how to manage your albums and expand their potential. Here are some tips for making the most of your albums:

- **Develop a naming system.** Names may include an initial (to indicate who took the pictures), the date or season, and the subject. If you use abbreviations consistently, you'll be able to identify your various albums at a glance.

- **Use albums as an organizational tool for your saved photos.** Add the photos you want to save to your albums in small groupings, giving the albums appropriate names. This may help you when it's time to clean house.
- **Remember that any changes you make to an album are visible by all who have access to it.** You can use this to your advantage by adding new pictures to an album and letting others know that the album has been updated. Of course, if you delete photos from an album, these photos will also be inaccessible to others unless they've already saved them.
- **To add a personal touch to your album, use the Upload Picture feature to include a personalized image in the album.** Try using your favorite graphics program to create an image with an introductory note, captioned photo, or fancy title (see Figure 5-5).
- **If you need to delete an album, click the My Albums tab, select the album you want to delete, and click the Delete button.** After you confirm the deletion, your album is removed and inaccessible to you and anyone with whom you shared it. Note, however, that deleting an album does not delete the photos within it; you delete individual pictures in the Saved Pictures area.

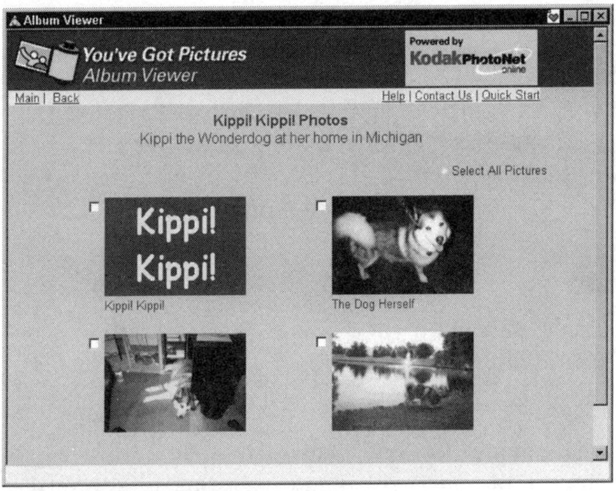

Figure 5-5. An album with a personalized image.

Places to Share Pictures

You've just taken an amazing shot of Cal Ripken at the moment he hit that 11th-inning home run. You already showed it off to your friends and family by e-mail or in an album. Now you want to show it off to the world! Where can you go to share pictures with others who enjoy good pictures? You'll find a wide variety of forums on AOL and the Internet where you can upload or otherwise submit your photo to share with others.

The "You've Got Pictures" Community Area

The "You've Got Pictures" community leaders host an area where you can submit your favorite photos. Your photo may even be chosen for picture of the week! Regular contests are sponsored through the *Picture This!* newsletter, too. To reach the community area, go to AOL Keyword: **Picture Community** or click on the Main Page link from within "You've Got Pictures."

Pet of the Day

The perfect place to submit your perfect pet photo is the Pet of the Day area (AOL Keyword: **Pet of the Day**), shown in Figure 5-6. Click the Nominate Your Pet Here link to learn how to send in your pet's photo and story.

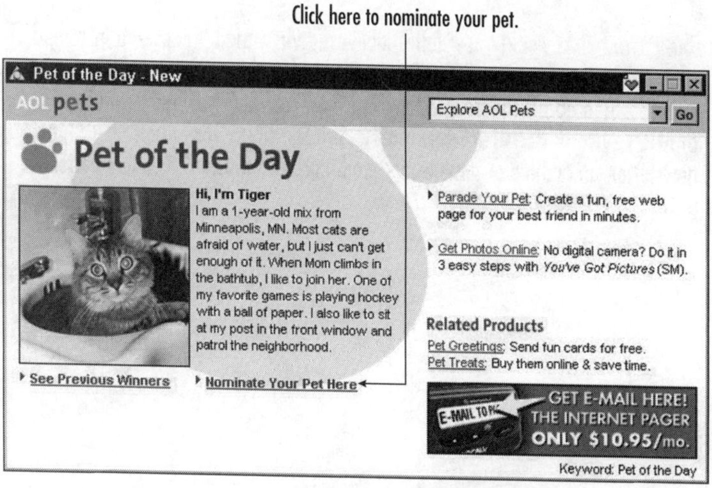

Figure 5-6. What better way to show off your pet to the world?

Love@AOL Photo Personals

If you're more interested in showing off your pretty face than your pet's, try Love@AOL's Photo Personals (AOL Keyword: **Photo Personals**). You can create a personal and include a photo of yourself with it! Click the Create a Personal button to learn how to create your personal profile and upload a photo for it.

Family Photo Contest

Submit that great photo of your family in the Family Photo Contest (Keyword: **Family Photo Contest**), sponsored by Kodak and ritzcamera.com. Contests are held regularly and often revolve around holidays such as Father's Day and special events.

Garden Gallery

Want to share your photo of a prized rose? Visit Keyword: **Garden Gallery** to upload a photo and share it with other nature lovers. Members can even vote on their favorite photos here.

Image Exchange

Photographers will enjoy the Image Exchange, an artist's community with thousands of images. Upload your photography to the Member Showcase, where up to 8 million people can ooh and ahh over your masterpiece. Use AOL Keyword: **Image Exchange**.

Find It Online

The *Picture This!* weekly newsletter, delivered via e-mail, keeps you informed of goings-on in the "You've Got Pictures" world, including places to post your pictures. Sign up for the newsletter from the "You've Got Pictures" main page at AOL Keyword: **Picture Community**. You can find information about the newsletter, an archive of newsletters, and links to Snapshot!, the newsletter's picture of the week.

Photo Libraries

Libraries where you can upload photos abound on AOL. Here are some favorites:

- The Grandstand (AOL Keyword: **Grandstand**) offers file libraries for all your favorite sports. For instance, the Motor Sports forum (AOL Keyword: **GS Auto**), part of Grandstand, has a Motor Sports library where you can upload your race-car photos and view others' photos.
- The Independent Traveler (AOL Keyword: **Traveler**) offers several libraries where you can upload your best vacation photos.
- The Graphic Arts Community (AOL Keyword: **Graphics**) lets you upload photos to the Graphics Arts Libraries for others to search and download. Read the Upload Guidelines carefully.

Chapter 6

Sharing Your Photos on Web Pages

In This Chapter

- Seeing what you can do with a Web page
- Presenting your pictures on the Web
- Creating your Web page with Easy Designer
- Finding your place at AOL Hometown

You're no doubt familiar with the World Wide Web. Web addresses — *h-t-t-p* this and *dot-com* that — are as common as, well, photographs. And even if you've considered the Web a fad or never considered that you'd need your own Web page, consider the following ways that you can use your digital pictures online:

- Provide potential employers with a digital version of your résumé enhanced by your digital picture.
- Promote a home business to your customers or potential customers with a page containing pictures of your products (and a few happy customers).
- Show the latest pictures of yours kids to your friends and extended family.
- Share pictures related to your interests with like-minded people through AOL Hometown.

AOL makes getting started on a Web page so easy that it's worth the effort to think through your purposes, gather materials, choose your tools, and otherwise get prepared to present your pictures through a Web page.

Gathering Your Thoughts and Web Page Content

You can mentally outline your Web page by answering the following questions:

- **What is the purpose of your page?** Purpose is the most important factor for grabbing your readers attention in any Web page or *Web site* (collection of pages). Purposes don't have to be serious, but they do need to be clear. Give your page a title that matches its purpose.
- **What sort of impression do you want to make?** Given your purpose, what personality do you want to project — professional, knowledgeable, welcoming, whimsical, or something else?
- **How important is visual interest?** Determine what visual elements — color, digital pictures, text areas, and so on — will support your pages' purpose and personality.
- **Where will the content come from?** Do the pictures and words you need exist, or must you either create them or collect them elsewhere?

Don't sweat the details if you don't have specific design ideas at this point. You can always use one of AOL's thematic, fill-in-the-blank templates to get started and then alter things to your liking later. Editing is easy with AOL's Web-publishing tools.

Tip

Most people who create Web pages continuously learn from each other's work. On AOL, the place to start to see others' work is AOL Hometown (AOL Keyword: **Hometown**), a small city, with many neighborhoods, for Web pages.

Gathering and Preparing Digital Pictures

Early in the Web-page-building process, you'll want to gather any digital pictures (along with any text) that you want to include in your page. The first step in gathering your digital pictures is to create a new folder or folders to hold them. For each Web page, consider creating a special folder for all your text and pictures.

Cross-Reference

You can download pictures from "You've Got Pictures" or from a digital camera or scanner into the folders you've created to hold your Web content. See Chapter 4 for information on how to download pictures from "You Got Pictures" that have the correct file format (GIF or JPG) to go on your Web page.

If you have any pictures or artwork in unusual file formats, convert them right away to GIFs or JPGs. To do this, you may need to use graphics software such as Paint Shop Pro or ThumbsPlus. Programs like these will both open your images and let you save them as GIFs or JPGs.

Choosing the Right Tool

AOL offers different tools for putting together your Web page; each tools takes a different approach.

- 1-2-3 Publish is the fastest way to create a page and publish it quickly in AOL Hometown. Choose a template, add your digital pictures and other content, put in some links, and you're done.
- Easy Designer gives you more flexibility and options than 1-2-3 Publish does. With Easy Designer, you can add pictures wherever you want, at whatever location on your page.
- You can use any Web page editor and upload the files to a special area (AOL Keyword: **My FTP Space**) and then add them to AOL Hometown from that area.

Choosing a tool does not necessarily prevent you from using a different tool. For example, if you start with 1-2-3 Publish, it is easy to continue editing the same page with Easy Designer. If you start with Easy Designer (which is described later in this chapter) however, you can't edit pages in 1-2-3 Publish.

Welcome to AOL Hometown

AOL Hometown provides a home on the World Wide Web for AOL members and nonmembers alike. Here's what you can find in this bustling virtual metropolis:

- **Web-publishing tools:** 1-2-3 Publish (super-easy) and Easy Designer (super-flexible), which simplify the creation of pages featuring your digital pictures.

- **A Web site:** Here, anyone can make any number of Web pages available. To make pages available simply means to copy your pages to Hometown, where they can be found and viewed by anyone with Web access.
- **Storage space:** AOL Hometown furnishes visitors with enough storage space to hold up to 12MB worth of digital pictures, Web pages, and anything else they want to make available to others.
- **Rich learning and reference resources:** AOL provides resources for learning the ropes of page-building, whether you're new to HTML (the language used to build Web pages) or want to acquire more advanced Web-building skills.

Creating Your Web Page with Easy Designer

AOL's new Web-publishing tool, Easy Designer (AOL Keyword: **Easy Designer**), offers more control of layout, page elements, and content than does 1-2-3 Publish. This extra functionality lets you lavish more attention on your creation. Now's the chance to add all those great digital pictures you've been salting away on your hard drive. When you're finished, store your Easy Designer page in AOL Hometown.

Tip: At AOL Hometown's Web-based message boards, you can ask questions and read answers to others' questions. Access these boards, as well as links to Web chats, by clicking the Talk About It link, on the opening page of AOL Keyword: **Hometown**. Or, you can always use the Easy Designer Help menu to get help on specific procedures.

Using a Template to Create a New Page

At the opening window of AOL Keyword: **Easy Designer**, you'll be asked whether you want to create a brand new page (click Create a New Page) or edit an existing page, such as a page started in 1-2-3 Publish (click Open an Existing Page).

- If you click the Create New Page link, your first job is to choose the template that best meets your needs. See Figure 6-1 for the templates at your disposal.

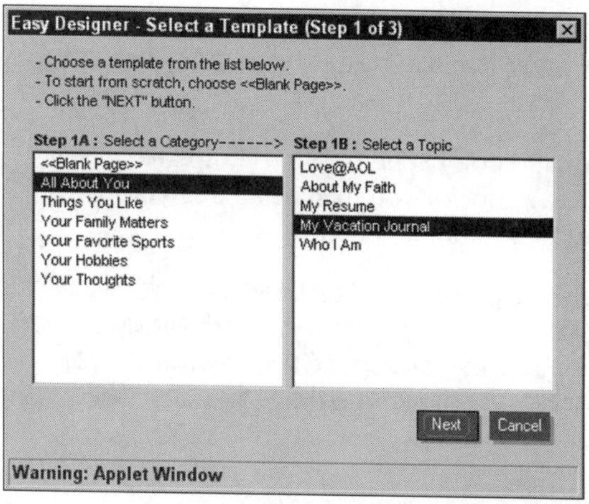

Figure 6-1. Select an Easy Designer category and topic, and you're ready to create your own page.

- With Easy Designer open, File⇨New likewise prompts you to select a template.
- You can choose Blank Page, an option shown at the top of the Select a Category list in Figure 6-1, if you want to start from scratch with your Web page design.

After clicking Create a New Page, follow these steps to create a Web page from a template in Easy Designer:

1. From the Easy Designer window (Figure 6-1), click a category (from the list on the left) and a topic (from the list on the right) that most closely match your needs. Click Next, and you go on to choose a page layout.
2. Click a layout that you want from the choices indicated by a series of thumbnail images. Notice that Easy Designer templates use multicolumn layouts and complex arrangements of text and pictures. Click Next.
3. Click a color scheme's name in the left side of the Select a Color window to see how the scheme looks in the right side. Click OK after selecting the color scheme that you want for your Web page.

Definition

A *color scheme* is a combination of colors designed to work together on your Web page: background color, text color, and a pair of colors for your visited links and unvisited links.

After selecting a layout and color scheme, your template appears (as shown in Figure 6-2), ready for you to start adding your own elements — digital pictures, links, and text.

Note

Don't worry if you later change your mind about the layout or color of your Web page. With your page displayed in Easy Designer, you can change layouts, move elements around on the page, add new elements, and so on. And at any time, you can click the Color button on the toolbar to change the color scheme or create a custom scheme.

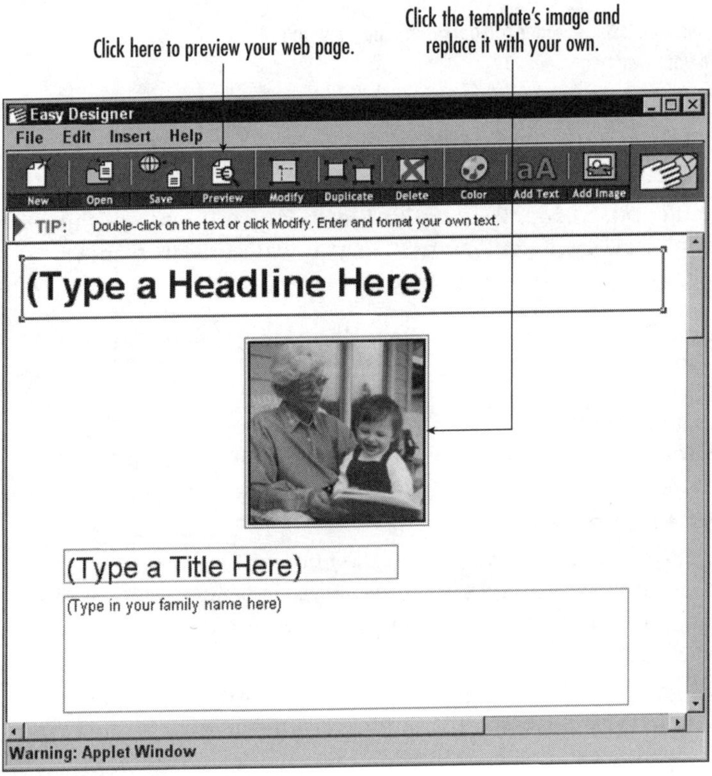

Figure 6-2. Your Web page template, ready to go.

4. After customizing your Web page, click Preview to see how your page looks before making it available on Hometown.
5. When you're happy with your page, click Save. After the page is saved, a message pops up informing you of its Web address.

Editing Digital Pictures in Easy Designer

When you use templates, you'll want to replace the template's images with your own pictures, as follows:

1. Select the digital picture you want to replace.
2. Click the Modify button on the Easy Designer toolbar.
3. In the resulting Picture Gallery box, click the Upload Picture button, as shown in Figure 6-3, to look for your own picture. (You can also look through Easy Designer's collection of more than 5,000 images to find one that might suit your needs.)
4. In the Upload Picture window, click Browse and find the desired digital picture on your hard drive. Click Upload Picture when you've selected the correct digital picture.

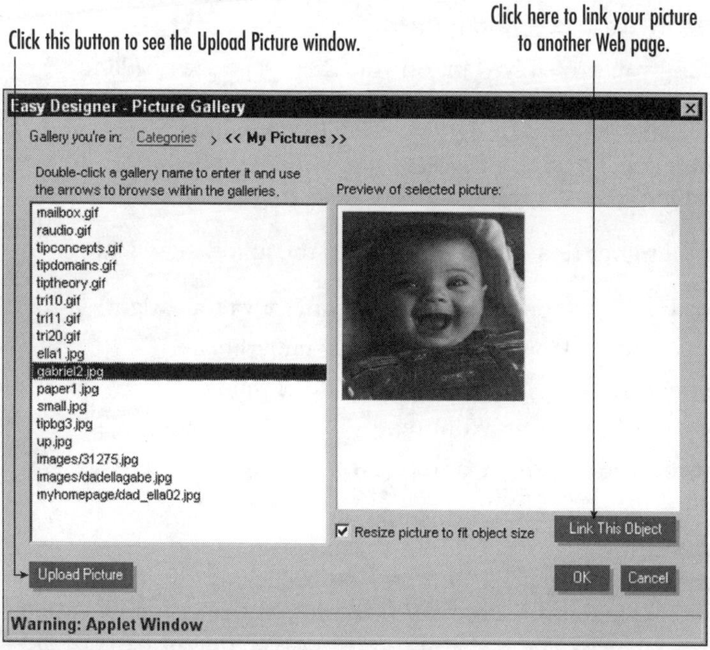

Figure 6-3. Choose a picture from your hard drive or the clip art and photo collection provided with Easy Designer.

Note If you find that the picture you uploaded appears on top of your heading (or other object), Easy Designer warns you with an `Overlap` warning message. Just drag the intruding object so that it's no longer overlapping other objects. You won't be able to save a page with overlapping elements.

Keep these other items in mind as you work with pictures on your Web page:

- Both the Text Editor and Picture Gallery window give you the ability to link your words or pictures to another Web page. This means that someone viewing your pages can click the linked text or picture to jump to a related page.
- You can resize a digital picture by simply selecting it and dragging one of its sides or a corner. Be careful not to distort it by changing its *aspect ratio* — the height and width relative to each other.
- You can also add a picture, including a picture still on your hard drive, by clicking the Add Image button and following the simple on-screen instructions.

Editing Text in Easy Designer

The first thing you probably want on your Web page is a headline. Double-click in the box where you see Type a Headline Here (or some similar message). The Easy Designer Text Editor window appears and lets you enter some text. You use the same window whether you're creating a headline or typing paragraphs of body text.

In the Easy Designer Text Editor, you can do the following:

- Add your own words and edit them until they're just right
- Style the text, making it **bold**, *italic*, or <u>underlined</u>
- Align the text along the right or left side of the box
- Change the font size and font type
- Adjust the size and shape of the text box

Just be sure to click OK when you're done!

You change the shape of a text box by simply clicking any side or corner and dragging in the direction you want. Notice also how your mouse arrow changes shape as you pass it across different parts of the box.

Tip

If you want to center the title of your page, clicking the Center button in the Text Editor is not enough. That action merely centers text in the box. You'll want to visually center the box on the page by moving it right and left until it *looks* centered between the Easy Designer window's right and left sides.

To edit the *contents* of any text box, double click inside the box. You can delete the existing text by selecting (highlighting) the text and pressing the backspace key. You can now add your own, new text, setting the font face, size, styling, and alignment as you wish. When you're done editing your text, click OK to close the Text Editor and return to Easy Designer.

Tip

For longer text blocks, consider writing and editing your text in a word processor (saving it if you want); you can then copy your words from the word processor and paste them into the text editor.

Editing a Published Easy Designer Page

Editing an Easy Designer Page is exactly like creating it in the first place: you use the same tools to do the same kinds of things.

To edit an Easy Designer page, you first retrieve the page. Go to AOL Keyword: **Easy Designer** and click the Open an Existing Page link to edit a published page. You need to know the page's filename in order to select it from the list that appears after you click Open Existing Page. Alternatively, if you know the published page's address, retrieve the published page itself, scroll down, and click the Easy Designer link at the bottom of the page.

1. From the Open Existing Page box, select a page and click Open.
2. The page opens in the Easy Designer window, which has the same buttons and works the same whether you're creating a new page or opening an existing one.
3. Right-click any block of text, digital picture, or other element, and you can choose to modify, duplicate, or delete it.
4. Click Save when you're done.

Here are some other useful tasks available from the Easy Designer toolbar (shown in Figure 6-4) that you can use when you're editing your page — and when you're building it in the first place:

- **Modify.** With an object selected, click this button to open the text or image editing window. Use the available tools to make any changes.

- **Duplicate.** This tool is handy if, for instance, you want to use the same graphical divider several times on the same page or repeat a tiny GIF bullet in a list. Instead of clicking Add Picture for each copied image, just highlight the box containing the picture or text to copy and click Duplicate. A copy of the object appears, and you can drag that copy to the place where you want it.
- **Delete.** Use this option to get rid of an unwanted object, for example a digital picture used in a template. Select the picture or other element; then click this button.
- **Color.** If you decide that your template's color scheme doesn't quite cut it, click this button to select another scheme or to create your own custom scheme. You can also add your own background image to your page.
- **Preview.** This button shows you the page as others will see it.
- **Save.** When you're happy with your page, this button lets you publish your page in AOL Hometown.

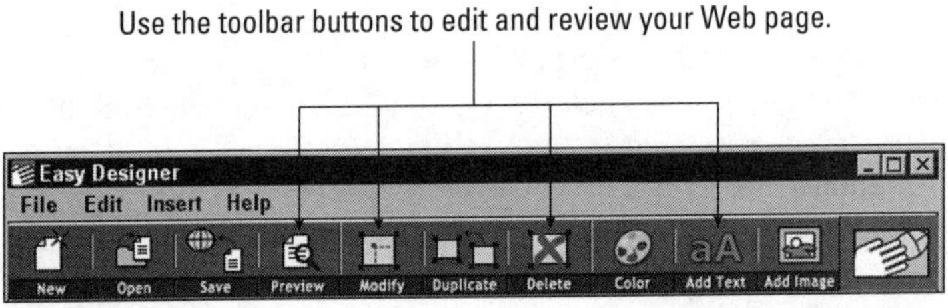

Figure 6-4. The Easy Designer toolbar.

When you finally save your new Easy Designer page, you will be notified first by the final Web page (after clicking Save) and then by e-mail of your new page's Web address. Your new Web address will be something like the following:

```
http://hometown.aol.com/YourScreenName/index.html
```

Note A **Web address**, or ***URL*** (short for Uniform Resource Locator), has several elements. In the example in the text: `http://` means that this is a Web page. `hometown.aol.com` tells the browser software *where* (on what Internet computer) the page can be found. The rest of the address says exactly where the page is on that computer (in what folder). It's like a path on your own hard drive, such as `c:/americaonline5.0/download/photos.exe`.

Adding Pages to AOL Hometown

When you create a page with either 1-2-3 Publish or Easy Designer, the page is automatically registered with Hometown AOL. The first thing to do with any *other* HTML page is to register it with AOL Hometown. With a page registered, people who either share your interests or know you personally stand a chance of finding your page. Being found is, well, the whole idea of creating a Web page.

Tip: You can register any pages with AOL Hometown, no matter how you created them. Add *all* your pages to AOL Hometown, and AOL gives you 12MB of storage space to use!

To expand your personal Web page offerings on AOL, go to the main AOL Hometown window (AOL Keyword: **Hometown**) and click the Add Pages link at the top of the page. From the Add & Manage Pages window, you can do the following:

- Add other pages (or *all* your pages) to AOL Hometown
- Move your pages from one AOL Hometown community to a different one
- Add and edit descriptions of pages, to make them easier to search for

Click Add Pages from just about anywhere in Hometown to get access to these choices. Adding your HTML pages to AOL Hometown takes (currently) five simple steps, which are well documented at every point on-screen. Remember that these are the pages made with visual editors other than 1-2-3 Publish and Easy Designer and then uploaded to My FTP Space.

1. AOL shows you all the pages you have uploaded to My FTP Space. Select the one you want to add. You can add several pages, but you must add them one at a time. Click Next to open a new window.
2. Write descriptive text about the page, if you want, and then click Next.
3. Select a category. Hometown AOL currently has such categories as Business, Careers, Culture, Education, Entertainment, Family, Food, and Hobbies. Click Next.

Tip: Make sure that you register the `index.htm` page (the default name of a page made by 1-2-3 and Easy Designer, and the default page opened when someone types in a URL but leaves off the specific file name, as in `www.aol.com`). This page also has links to all your other pages. That way, people who find your page on Hometown AOL will view it the way you intended.

4. Select the subcategory where your page best fits. Click Next.
5. Select a community within that subcategory that would make the best home for your page. Click Next to plant your page in a suitable Hometown community.

Note: Moving pages from one community to another involves an almost identical process.

Finding Other People's Pages in Hometown AOL

While you create your own pages, other AOL members are creating Web pages devoted to their sundry passions and possessions. AOL has already opened 1-2-3 Publish and Easy Designer to anyone on the Internet, giving members and non-members alike the opportunity to add pages to any of the AOL Hometown communities, where they are searchable.

You can search AOL Hometown pages for key words or phrases — words used in people's descriptions of their own pages. Or, you can search for pages created by a particular screen names.

Tip: Whenever you stumble across an AOL Hometown page that you especially like, you can tell a friend about it by clicking E-Mail This Page (at the top of your page), which summons up a fill-in-the-blank form. Enter one or more recipients' e-mail addresses, type your message, and click Send. The clickable link will be automatically included in the message. Take advantage of this easy way to notify your friends when you create a Web page.

The Hometown AOL home page (directly available at AOL Keyword: **Hometown** or at `hometown.aol.com`) puts these search techniques at your fingertips. To search pages by key word or screen name, type a screen name or key word into the Search Pages box at AOL Hometown's opening page, then click Search. Next, you'll probably see a list of pages (if you don't, try modifying your search words). Click any page to visit it directly. In addition to searching at AOL Keyword: **Hometown**, you can also browse AOL Hometown by burrowing through categories and subcategories and on to communities in quest of the pages that interest you.

Tip: What are others doing on Hometown? Check out each week's Top Picks, available from AOL Keyword: **Hometown**. From Hometown's opening page, click Member Hall of Fame for the best of the best.

Chapter 7

Turning Your Photos into Prints and Gifts

In This Chapter

- Ordering prints through "You've Got Pictures"
- Getting your photos onto gift items like T-shirts and mugs
- Using Quick Checkout to speed things up
- Sending photo greeting cards

Whether they're carefully mounted in a frame on top of the piano or taped to the refrigerator door, photographic prints make a great gift for you or anyone else in your life. And anyone with whom you've shared your pictures by e-mail or Buddy Album can also order prints and gifts from "You've Got Pictures."

Ordering Prints

You can order prints in three sizes: 4 x 6 inches (the traditional jumbo snapshot size) for $0.49 each, 5 x 7 inches for $1.49 each, and 8 x 10 inches for $4.49 each (all prices are subject to change). The minimum charge is $3.00, so you'll want to order more than one of the smaller-sized prints.

Here's how you and the people you share pictures with can order prints:

1. While viewing pictures in any tab (New Rolls, Saved Pictures, My Albums, or Buddy Albums), click the Order Prints & Gifts button to go to the Picture Store.
2. Click the Prints button.
3. At the top of the Order Prints page, shown in Figure 7-1, select a print size (4 x 6, 5 x 7, or 8 x 10) and then indicate which picture(s) you want to have printed. Alongside each image in the

album is a text box in which you can indicate the quantity of prints you want of each image.

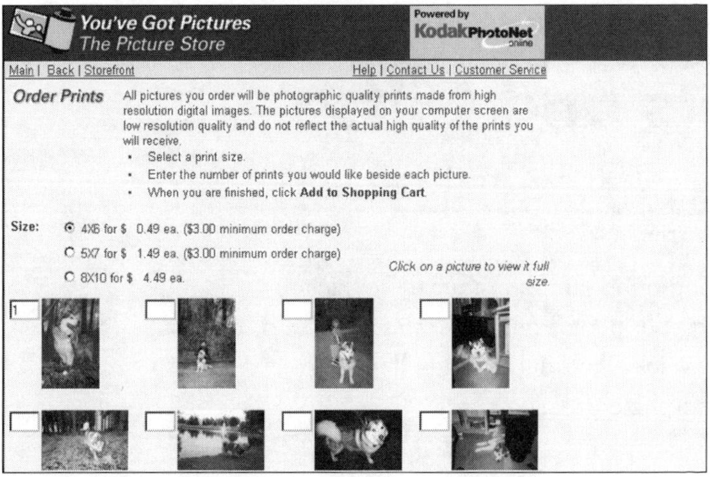

Figure 7-1. Select the picture(s) you want to have printed.

To order prints in other sizes or from other albums, you have to make those selections later in the ordering process.

Note "You've Got Pictures" prints your photos on high-quality photographic paper. However, the overall quality of the image depends on many factors, including the resolution of the original image (in pixels) and the size of the print you order. Pictures processed by "You've Got Pictures" are stored at a resolution of 1536 x 1024 pixels. To most casual observers this resolution provides very good results at 4 x 6 and 5 x 7 inches, and acceptable results at 8 x 10 inches. If you uploaded digital pictures created at a lower resolution (such as 768 x 512), the free, middle-grade download from "You've Got Pictures," larger prints will likely be less satisfactory.

4. When you've finished selecting pictures from this album, click the Add to Shopping Cart button at the bottom of the page. If you'd rather select prints from another album, click the Choose Another Album button at the bottom of the page (any selections you made in the current album will be ignored).

When you click the Add to Shopping Cart button, you see a list of all the prints you've ordered so far as well as a thumbnail image of each, as shown in Figure 7-2.

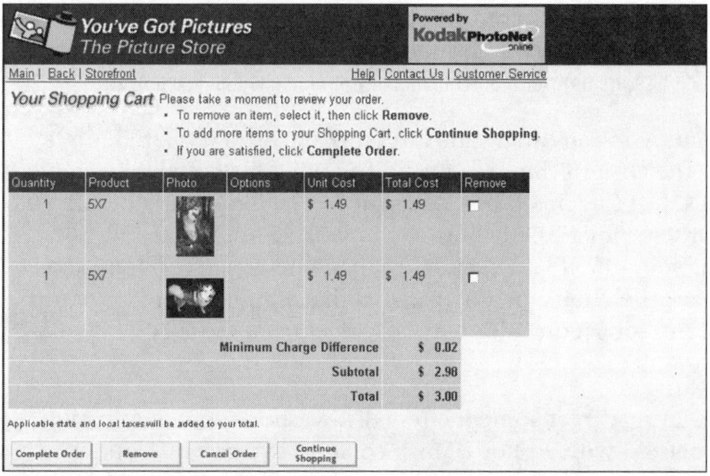

Figure 7-2. The shopping cart displays your selections.

You can remove photos from the shopping cart, continue shopping, cancel your order, or, when you're finished, click the Complete Order button. If you want more prints, click the Continue Shopping button to return to the Picture Store. From there, you can order more prints or prints of other sizes, or any number of other gifts.

Choosing Photo Gifts

Photo gifts are an ideal way to showcase that favorite photo in a manner that's both practical and personal. You can make a gift for yourself or send it to a friend, family member, or co-worker. In fact, a photo gift may be the just the thing for someone who has everything.

Tip

Non-AOL members can also order picture gifts featuring the photographs that they've received from AOL members. Non-AOL members who receive a Buddy Album notification can go to `pictures.aol.com` and sign in using their user name and password. From there, they select the picture they want to use and click the Order Prints & Gifts button.

Photo gifts are normally shipped within five business days following receipt of your order, but if it will take longer than five days, you're notified by e-mail and given an opportunity to cancel your order. Gifts are shipped U.S. First Class Mail and should arrive within 7 to 14 days after you place your order.

Note: Shopping online is reliable, safe, and secure. AOL is committed to providing members with the most advanced, up-to-date security technology by incorporating a secure browser that scrambles any information that you provide.

As with prints, you can order gifts directly from "You've Got Pictures" by clicking the Order Prints & Gifts button when you're viewing a picture. If you select the check box adjacent to a single picture before you click the Order Prints & Gifts button, that image is automatically selected for your gift. If you click more than one image (or none at all), you later have the choice of any image in that album. From the Picture Store window (see Figure 7-3), you can select from the following gift items:

- **Photo mugs:** Treat someone to a dishwasher-safe, ceramic mug personalized with a photo. Mugs come in two sizes: 11 ounce and 15 ounce and display pictures in landscape view (wide) or portrait view (tall).

Tip: Order a mug with a photo of each member of your family or office staff. The photo on the mug will help each person identify his or her mug. It may also encourage folks to clean out their own mugs!

- **Puzzles:** Send your friend a special puzzle — one that, when assembled, turns out to be a picture of a loved-one. This puzzle won't challenge jigsaw-puzzle fanatics. It measures 10½ x 15 inches and has only 80 pieces, but there's still lots of room for friendly fun for around $17.
- **Mouse pads:** Maybe your favorite nature picture would look great as a mouse pad. The "You've Got Pictures" mouse pad measures 8 x 9½ inches, costs about $14, and has the traditional non-slip rubber backing and cloth top.
- **Bears:** Perhaps that special person in your life will appreciate a teddy bear wearing a photo T-shirt! This is a great Valentine's Day item and makes an especially cute gift for a baby's room — a very special way to display a newborn's portrait.
- **Clothing:** Photo T-shirts and sweatshirts are versatile gift items. From proud grandparents sporting their newest grandchild to a project leader looking to build team spirit, anyone can think of a way to customize a T-shirt. Your picture is printed on the front of a 100-percent cotton T-shirt for about $20, or on a 50-percent cotton blend sweatshirt for about $26. You have your choice of fabric colors (as long as it's white), and shirts are available in seven sizes, from children's small to adult extra-large.

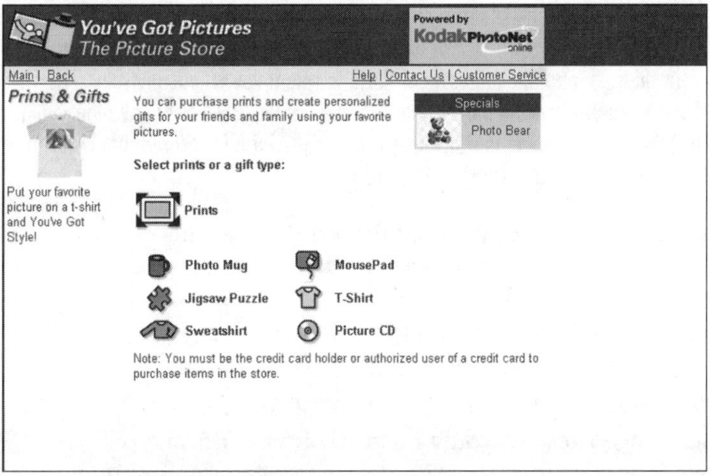

Figure 7-3. The Picture Store offers prints and much more..

How to Order from "You've Got Pictures"

To order a photo gift, follow these simple steps:

1. Locate the photo you want to use at AOL Keyword: **Pictures**.
2. Select the check box next to the desired photo. If you select more than one, you'll be asked to reselect just one photo later in the process.
3. Click the Order Prints & Gifts button.
4. On the next page that appears, click the icon of the item on which you want your photo to appear. Another new page displays the selected product, a thumbnail-sized version of the selected photo, and size and quantity options.
5. Click the Change Photo button to select another image, select any other options that you want, and click the Add to Shopping Cart button. Yet another page appears, displaying the contents of your shopping cart (refer to Figure 7-2).
6. Review your order. To remove something (or everything) from your shopping cart, select the Remove check box adjacent to that item and click the Remove button. You can then click the Continue Shopping button or the Cancel Order button, or if you're ready to pay for your purchases, click the Complete Order button.

Tip

To speed up your online purchasing, you may want to sign up for AOL Quick Checkout, which securely stores information for up to ten of your credit cards, your address, and the addresses of those to whom you frequently send gifts. Then when you make a purchase at "You've Got Pictures" or at any other online merchant participating in Quick Checkout, you'll finish in record time. Visit AOL Keyword: **Quick Checkout** to find out more.

7. On the next page, enter your billing and shipping information and then click the Continue button. The next page summarizes your order information.
8. Click the Change button if you need to make any changes, or click the Continue button. You're still free to click the Cancel button if you've changed your mind about your order.
9. The next page presents you with your order confirmation number. It doesn't hurt to *write it down* or print it out. You will also receive an e-mail containing your confirmation number and detailed help instructions.

Completing the Transaction

AOL goes to great lengths to make your online shopping experience simple and safe. All transactions are encrypted and secure if you're using AOL 3.0 and higher software and if you're using the browser supplied with that software. If, by some small chance, you do fall victim to credit card fraud, AOL provides coverage for your loss. You must report the fraud to your credit card company, and AOL will then pay up to an additional $50 for any remaining liability for the unauthorized charges.

Caution

Never give your credit card information or password to unauthorized persons contacting you via e-mail or Instant Message. These requests are always fraudulent. AOL will never ask you for this information using these methods.

Because your "You've Got Pictures" purchases are customized, your return privileges are limited. Obviously, you're covered if your order is damaged or if there is a discrepancy in your order (check your order carefully when you receive it). You can also receive a full refund if your order is not 100 percent free from defects in materials and workmanship. Be sure to save the original packing materials and file your claim within 30 days of receipt.

Note

Neither AOL nor its affiliates will ever ask you for your credit card number (except during initial AOL registration or when you're actually making a purchase online).

When you're in the "You've Got Pictures" store, you'll find handy hyperlinks at the top of each page for Help, Contact Us, and Customer Service. Review these areas before you place your first order. You'll feel much better about the entire process.

Sending Photo Greeting Cards

American Greetings (AOL Keyword: **AG**) operates a huge online service site offering free online greeting cards (the kind that are sent via e-mail and viewed in a Web browser). Now when you send an online greeting, you can upload your own picture to accompany the card. Depending on the occasion, you may want to send a picture of yourself, a picture of your newborn baby, or a picture of your new home so folks will recognize it when they come to your housewarming party.

Tip

AG's online greetings are also available whenever you write an AOL e-mail message (click Write on the AOL toolbar). In the Write Mail window, the new Greetings button, which used to be called Mail Extras, offers choices of pictures, drawings, and sounds to use in your messages. Click Greetings for the AG Web page. There, you can select an online greeting, which will be sent instantly.

Follow these steps to send a photo greeting card:

1. Download a picture to your hard drive (if it's not already there). The image file must be less than 50K (kilobytes) in size, so you should download an E-Mail & Web Page Quality image; higher-quality downloads are too large.
2. Go to AOL Keyword: **AG**.
3. In the Online Greetings area, select an online greeting card and fill in the Personalize Your Greeting form, along with your choice of font and font color. You can also choose the date on which you want the card delivered.
4. In the Add a Photo section at the bottom of the page for your chosen card, click the Browse button and then select the picture file of your choice from your hard drive. You're then asked to verify that you own the right to use the photo and to agree to American Greetings' Terms of Service.

5. Click the Send Your Greeting button. Your recipient will receive an e-mail invitation to view the card on the Web. When viewing the card, that person sees a big View My Photo button alongside the regular greeting card.

Other Sources of Photo Goodies

Photofinisher Wolf Camera, a participating "You've Got Pictures" photo dealer, offers a variety of gifts at its Web site `www.wolfcamera.com`. In addition to products similar to those offered by "You've Got Pictures," you can order tote bags, aprons, neckties, hats, photo albums, and buttons, all decorated with your digital pictures.

In addition to the wide choice of goodies, Wolf can produce photo enlargements from digital files up to 12 x 18 inches ("You've Got Pictures" goes up to 8 x 10 inches).

On the downside, Wolf recommends a print resolution of 1164 x 1528 pixels to produce a good 12-x-18-inch print! P.A.W.S. also requires that you download and install a separate program (PC and Mac versions are available) to use the service.

Appendix A

Digital Imaging Terms and Concepts

Glossary of Terms

album

A collection of digital pictures.Albums can be used to organize your digital pictures and to share them with others. Many home image-editing programs let you make digital photo albums.

analog

A way of representing information in a format that attempts to reproduce real sounds, images, and movement by capturing (for example) a sound wave's differing levels and properties.An example of analog technology is a film camera, which captures a scene's continuity of color with a high degree of fidelity. See also *digital.*

archive

Files grouped for a purpose: to be compressed, transmitted, stored, or simply made available for viewing by others.Also, a collection of digital pictures on your hard drive or other storage device.

attachment

A digital picture, word-processing document, or other file sent with an e-mail message.When you use the built-in e-mail program in "You've Got Pictures," digital pictures are sent as attachments.

bit

Short for *binary unit,* also know as *digit.* The basic unit of computer storage, a digit can only be a 0 or 1.

bit depth

Describes the number of colors (or shades of gray) that any pixel can display and hence the number of bits needed to record this. If eight bits are used to define a pixel's color, the pixel can display up to 256 colors. If 24 bits are used, more than 16 million colors can be displayed. Reducing bit depth is a simple way to reduce the size of files intended for Web use.

bitmap

A type of graphic file that stores information about colors and tones in small blocks called pixels. BMP, JPG, and GIF files are made up of bitmaps. See also *Vector graphics.*

BMP

A file saved in a standard Windows file format for graphics.

byte

A unit of computer-readable data made up of eight binary digits or bits. Typically defines a single character, such as a letter or symbol, but can store other information. A byte is the standard measure of file size (amount of space it takes up on a hard drive or other storage medium).

CD-R (compact disc recordable)

Optical digital storage drive that lets you save files on a CD. CD-R disks can only be *written to* once. See also *CD* and *CD-RW.*

CD-RW (compact disc rewritable)

A new type of optical digital storage drive that lets you save files on the same CD many times, as you do with floppy diskettes or tapes. See also *CD-R.*

clip art

A collection of digital images included with many common software applications and designed for use in Web sites, graphic presentations, and other documents.

CMYK

Shorthand used in printing to describe any color as a combination of four different ink colors: cyan, magenta, yellow, and black. Used to describe colors for print publications. See also *RGB.*

contrast

Range of brightness between the light and dark areas of a photograph or other graphic image; a high-contrast image has a wide range.

crop

To trim a photograph or other graphic image down to the portion you want to edit, print, or display.

database

Structured and searchable collection of data in the true sense of data — discrete bits of information. Database products like Filemaker and Microsoft Access can be used to organize your digital pictures.

digital

A way of representing complex images, sounds, video, and text (and more) into computer-readable patterns of binary numbers (1s and 0s). The purpose of digitizing is to make extremely diverse types of information (1) widely available to people and (2) easily manipulable and transmissible by computers. See also *analog.*

digital camera

A camera that captures images digitally rather than on film, using a charge-coupled device (CCD) and computer memory. The digital pictures can be downloaded as files to a computer, where they can be edited, shared, and used in many ways.

download

To transfer information from one computer to another, usually from a remote networked computer such as a Web server to a personal computer, but also from other devices (such as cameras and scanners) to a PC.

dpi (dots per inch)

A way of measuring the resolution (sharpness, or amount of information conveyed) especially for printers and scanners. If yon know an image's overall resolution in pixels, settings its dots (or pixels) per inch determines how big on a monitor or page it will be.

file compression

Storing a file in a format that reduces its file size to speed up transmission and reduce storage requirements. JPG files, a common graphics format, can be compressed to download more quickly.

file format

A standard manner in which certain types of files are stored that enables software to determine what application is needed to open the file. The format is usually represented by a file extension following the filename, such as `.TXT` (text files), `.BMP` (bit-mapped graphics), `.JPG`, and `.GIF` (standard bit-mapped graphic formats for use on the Web).

filters

(1) Electronic filters are common in photo manipulation programs like Adobe Photoshop and MGI PhotoSuite III to provide image-editing enhancements and special effects.

FTP (File Transfer Protocol)

A standard method for transmitting files from one computer to another via the Internet. Often used to share large files or upload HTML files from a personal computer to a Web server.

GIF (Graphics Interchange Format)

A graphics file format common on the Internet and nearly universally supported by browsers. It can be formatted to enable a transparent image background, making it useful for Web pages. Most commonly used for solid-colored images, logos, buttons, cartoons, and similar, simple images.

grayscale

A black-and-white representation of an image that can include many shades of gray.

hard drive

Primary file storage hardware on a PC. Uses magnetic storage media.

HTML (HyperText Markup Language)

The script (code) used to format ASCII text files into documents usable by a Web browser; browsers download HTML files and display them as Web pages.

image map

A *single* Web graphic that provides a *set* of links to different destinations.

interpolated (also enhanced or inferred) resolution

Optical scanner resolution fine-tuned with software to produce the effect of additional pixels and thus a sharper image. See also *pixel (picture element).*

JPEG or JPG (Joint Photographic Experts Group)

A graphics file format widely used on the Web. Compresses well, enabling transmission of large, complex graphics such as photographs, with more or less loss of image quality depending on the amount of compression.

LCD (liquid crystal display)

A type of display commonly used on laptop monitors, digital camera viewers, and other types of hardware. On digital cameras, an LCD viewer usually lets you (1) view a scene before it's captured, (2) an image after its captured, and (3) a menu of choices for setting exposure and managing pictures.

lens

Ground glass, sometimes plastic, that focuses light on film or, in a digital camera, the CCD surface (see *digital camera*). Also used to describe a group of lenses that function as a unit, as is the case with most camera lenses.

megapixel

A way of measuring the maximum resolution of a camera's digital-picture files. A megapixel camera records more than 1 million pixels in an image, usually by recording at least 1152 pixels long by 872 pixels wide. The resulting files are often required for good printout quality but are usually excessive for good Web quality. Some current cameras now top 3 megapixels.

My FTP Space

Online storage provided for AOL members, based on *FTP.* Used for storing Web files and other documents meant for sharing with other people on the Internet. AOL Keyword: **My FTP Space**.

optical resolution

Actual physical resolution that a scanner or printer is capable of recording in dots per inch (dpi). See also *dpi (dots per inch).*

PDF (Portable Document Format)

Created by Adobe, a popular file format used to present highly formatted documents, especially as word-processing documents, to publish on the Web. The Adobe Acrobat reader is freely available at `www.adobe.com`, but to create Acrobat documents, you must purchase the full Adobe Acrobat software.

pixel (picture element)

The smallest unit of a bitmapped (standard) digital image, a small square made up of a specific color. The resolution (sharpness) of monitors, scanners, and digital cameras is measured in terms of the number of pixels across by pixels down (monitor); or dots (same as pixels) per inch (printer), or pixels per image (digital picture). The number of colors a pixel can display depends on its color depth, determined by the number of bits used to define a color for any pixel. See *bitmap.*

removable media

Computer storage consisting of a drive (usually the personal computer, with a slot) and removable storage units such as floppies, Zip disks, or writable CDs.

resolution

The sharpness or fineness of a digital picture, either printed or onscreen, usually as measured by the number of pixels in the image file. Also describes the sharpness a monitor can display, a printer can output, or a scanner can capture.

RGB

A way of defining colors as combinations of red, green, and blue light, for on-screen use (since screens are lit from behind by moving beams of light). See also *CMYK*.

scanner

A piece of hardware that converts a paper-based text or image, such as a photo or document, into a digital file that can be manipulated by using image-editing software or used on a Web page or elsewhere online.

screen capture

A digital picture showing all or part of whatever is displayed on a computer monitor.

screen resolution

Measures the number of pixels that appear on your monitor, usually as a vertical by horizontal measure, such as 640 by 480. Most monitors let you set resolution at various levels; the higher the *resolution,* the smaller but sharper any individual image appears on-screen.

selection tools

In image editing software, selection tools allow you to identify the part of an image to which you want to apply effects and changes, protecting the rest of the image in the process. Common selection tools include rectangular and elliptical, magic wand, and freehand (also known as lasso).

serial port

A plug at the back of your computer that you use to attach a cable to modems, digital cameras, and other devices. Today, the USB port has superseded the serial port for many uses.

slide show

AOL and other software publishers use the term *slide show* to describe the display of a series of pictures, often accompanied by sound. Microsoft PowerPoint is used to create slide shows, and many image-editing programs (including MGI PhotoSuite III and ThumbsPlus) create slide shows based only on your digital pictures.

SLR (Single Lens Reflex camera)

Common camera type in which you compose a photograph through the actual lens that will take the picture. SLRs often use interchangeable lenses (of different zoom capabilities and *focal lengths*). Digital cameras that are comparable in quality and features to traditional film SLRs remain prohibitively expensive.

still

A single frame of a video clip. Like digital pictures, stills capture a moment. A digital video camera, however, stills lack the clarity and compositional controls of a digital picture.

stock photos

Collections of digital pictures made available for publication or other use, often for a fee. Many such services are available over the Web.

thumbnail

A small version of a digital image, viewed on-screen. Often used to ease locating and organizing graphics files by allowing multiple images to be viewed on-screen simultaneously.

TIF (Tagged Image File)

A graphics file format used with both Windows and Mac operating systems that retains a great deal of image information but at the cost of producing large files.

TWAIN (from "never the twain shall meet")

Software that lets you import an image from a scanner or digital camera directly into a graphics application. What this means is that you control key hardware functions, such as downloading pictures from a digital scanner or initiating a scan, from within the software.

underexposure

Application of less light to capture a photographic image than a light meter reports as necessary. Can be used intentionally to alter the image or compensate for difficult lighting situations that may result in meter error.

upload

To transfer a file from your personal computer to another (usually larger) computer. On AOL, you use AOL Keyword: **My FTP Space** to upload files for anyone with Internet access to *download.*

USB (Universal Serial Bus) port

A newer personal computer plug designed for nearly any peripheral device. USB devices, such as printers and scanners, can be plugged into each other. Most digital cameras can use USB ports, but require a special, inexpensive cable to do so.

vector graphics

Graphic image files saved as mathematical formulas to represent lines and shapes, by using a continuous line rather than a series of pixels as with bitmapped graphics. Web pages display bitmapped graphics (JPGs and GIFs). To construct vector graphics, you need to use a special graphics program such as Adobe Illustrator, Macromedia Freehand, or CorelDRAW.

viewfinder

On a traditional or digital camera, the window that you look through when composing your picture. Usually differs slightly from the actual area captured in a photo. Most digital cameras offer an LCD viewfinder in additional to a standard viewfinder.

wide angle lens

A lens with a shorter-than-normal focal length and wide field of view.

WYSIWIG (What You See Is What You Get)

Pronounced "whizzy-wig." Used to describe a graphical software user interface in which the editing view closely approximates the final printed or on-screen appearance.

Zip

(1) A generic term for file compression. (2) Extension of a set of zipped files. (3) A Zip drive is a type of storage medium that holds more data than a floppy, 100MB or 250MB, instead of 1.5MB.

zoom

(1) In photography, changing the lens's focal length to see more or less of the subject. (2) In image-editing software, you zoom into a picture to do fine edits and zoom out to view the overall image.

zoom lens

A lens with a variable focal length, letting you capture more or less of the main subject.

Understanding Digital Images

Software for enhancing your digital pictures brings the control and creativity of the darkroom to the living room, and you won't have to breathe the fumes. With inexpensive graphics software, you can now remove red eye from your digital photos, turn up the contrast on washed-out scenes, and tune down the shadows in those unevenly exposed beach scenes. To use the software effectively, it helps to understand the basic relations between resolution, picture size, and file size.

Resolution and Picture Size

Resolution and picture size are closely linked. With digital pictures, *resolution* usually refers to how sharp an image looks as measured by pixels (picture elements) per image. *In general,* the more pixels per image, the finer the detail collected (and the better the image appears when printed on paper or shown on-screen).

Note: It's possible to change the size of a picture without changing the number of pixels in the image, which is why it's not always true that the more pixels per image the better the image's quality.

There are exceptions to the general rule. For example, you can change the size of the picture without changing the number of pixels. Just like spreading butter, the thinner you spread the same number of pixels, the fewer pixels for each part of the picture. To the eye, the spread-out image is going to appear more "pixelated" — show more jagged lines, less continuous colors and tones.

A picture's size in pixels also makes a difference when you're using the picture on a Web page or for any on-screen use:

- For on-screen use, big files have long download times for people viewing the picture. That's why you'll want to use far fewer dots per inch for the Web — 72 or 96 dpi (dots/pixels per inch) — as compared to 300 dpi for prints.

Tip: AOL 5.0 displays best at a screen resolution of 800 x 600 pixels or above. You adjust your screen resolution in Windows 95/98 by right-clicking the desktop, selecting Properties, opening the Settings tab, and moving the Desktop area lever to the right or left. When you have finished making adjustments, click Apply and then OK. Your screen may flicker momentarily, but don't worry.

- With a computer monitor's resolution unchanged, if you have two pictures to display, the picture with more pixels is simply going to need more space to display than one with fewer pixels. For example, a 640-by-480-pixel image appears larger than a 320-x-240-pixel image. If you have a megapixel version of the same image, it will be larger than your screen and you'll have to scroll to the left and right to see the whole thing.

Resolution and File Size

The resolution of an image file (in pixels) affects its file size (in kilobytes). A higher-resolution image (640 x 480 pixels, as in the AOL PhotoCam) must obviously be bigger than a 340 X 260 image — just to store all those extra pixels.

Think of what happens when you jump to the megapixel cameras and three-megapixel cameras! Although great for prints, they're not much use for many on-screen uses. Three or four 1152 x 872 digital photos can weigh in at a megabyte or so. When you remember that the average floppy disk can only hold 1.4MB, even a handy camera like the Sony Mavica, which stores pictures right on a floppy disk, will max out on a couple of these megapixel pictures.

Computers and Colors

In the world of magazines and four-color printing, colors are described as a mix of cyan (an intense light blue), magenta (a deep purplish red), yellow, and black ink. Each color can be defined as four numbers — one value each for C, M, Y, and K. The shorthand for this system of describing colors is CMYK — K is black.

Definition

Computers describe every color as a combination of red, green, and blue (RGB) light. Each main color can assume any of 256 values (for example, from no red to solid red), and you can use software to adjust the density and brightness of the color.

Computers, however, describe every color in terms of a different model: as combinations of red, green, and blue (RGB) light. For any combination of red, green, and blue, software lets you set values such as *saturation* (density of color, from washed out and gray to fully and intensively colored) and *luminosity* (brightness of the color).

What You Need to Know About Graphics Files

If you are planning to use your digital photographs in creative projects or on Web pages, it helps to get comfortable with file formats. This stuff reads like alphabet soup at first, but it becomes second nature quickly enough.

Tip

Excellent information about file types is available on AOL. At AOL Keyword: **Help**, click the A-Z index. Under F, read the article called About File Types and Extensions.

Digital pictures, like most kinds of computer files, can be saved in various standardized file formats. A file *format* is indicated by the *file extension,* which is the part of the *filename* that appears after the period. For example, the extensions JPG and GIF are the file formats indicated by filenames `beach.JPG` and `beach.GIF`. JPG and GIF are the two major graphics formats used on the Web. Based on the extension, your computer can usually figure out what program to use to open a file.

Tip

AOL has always offered members a way of viewing common graphics files, online and offline. With the AOL software open (but you don't have to sign on), choose File⇨Open. Browse to a specific JPG, GIF, or BMP file and double-click to view it. AOL's Picture Gallery lets you view all GIFs, JPGs, and BMPs in a specific folder.

JPG

Usually pronounced "jay-peg," this format has a fairly compact file size but a high image quality, making it a good format for photographs. JPGs are particularly good for the Web because they can be compressed (decreased in size), can be downloaded quickly, and can be viewed with any Web browser, including Netscape Navigator and the version of Internet Explorer included with AOL. (JPGs get their name from the Joint Photographic Experts Group, the organization that developed the format.)

GIF

Usually pronounced "giff" with a hard *G* (and less commonly as "jiff," like the peanut butter), this format provides a reasonably small file size compared to JPGs, partly because a GIF pixel can't represent as many colors as a JPG pixel. GIFs work better for solid colors and simple black, white, and gray images; JPGs are better suited for continuous-tone images such as photographs. GIFs are widely used on the Web for banners, line art, logos, and simple graphics. GIF stands for Graphic Interchange Format. Figure A-1 shows a JPG (the photo) and two GIFs (the logo and the button).

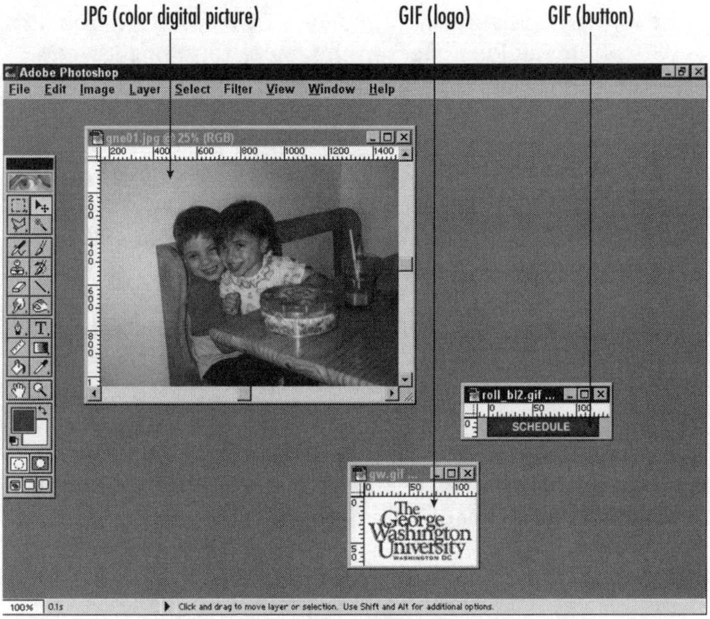

Figure A-1. This Photoshop image shows a GIF (simple black-and-white line drawing) and a JPG (color digital picture).

ART

ART is AOL's own file format. To download certain Web graphics more quickly, AOL's Web browser converts them into this format. The AOL Picture Gallery can display ART files and convert them into JPGs and GIFs for use in other programs. ART works by compressing certain Web graphics, sometimes at the loss of quality. To turn off the automatic conversion to ART: choose My AOL⇨Preferences from the AOL toolbar; click the WWW button; click the Web Graphics tab; make sure there's no check in the Use Compressed Graphics check box.

Editing Images with AOL Picture Gallery

AOL's Picture Gallery is built right into AOL 4.0 and higher. It lets you view your digital pictures and make some overall edits. Online or offline, Picture Gallery is available by choosing File⇨Open Picture Gallery. In the Open Picture Gallery window, browse to the folder with the images you want to edit and click the Open Gallery button. You'll see a screen with all the digital images in the folder, thumbnail-sized (small), six at a time. To see an individual image, just click it, and the image comes up in a new window.

Tip: The Revert button at the bottom of Picture Gallery enables you to go back to the last saved version of an image, removing all changes made since then — not just the last change. In Picture Gallery (or any other program), save after making any change you want to keep.

The Picture Gallery tools apply changes to the entire photograph, except for cropping, which (by definition) lets you remove those parts of a picture that don't add anything to your subject, creating, in effect, a new rectangular shape to hold your picture. These quick changes can improve photographs that weren't composed, exposed, or developed perfectly, and such changes can save you the effort of using more powerful but more cumbersome image-editing software.

Tip: Play around with Picture Gallery as with any image-editing software, but don't forget, to first save your file with a different filename!

Optimizing Web Graphics: File Format

Graphics on the Web need to be in GIF or JPG format, and each format has advantages for specific uses.

Preparing JPGs for the Web

Complex and colorful photos are best saved as JPGs. A JPG supports something called 24-bit color, meaning that each pixel can represent more than 16 million colors and the resulting images tend to look better. JPGs have another advantage: They can be *compressed* — reduced in file size for quick downloading. Compressing a JPG too much, however, causes its quality to deteriorate. Editing software such as Adobe PhotoShop and Macromedia Fireworks lets you determine the level of compression when you save a file as a JPG.

Tip

When selecting a JPG compression level (the process varies with software), start with a middle setting in a program; then zoom in to check the results. If the image deterioration is minimal, increase the compression and check again.

Preparing GIFs for the Web

Line art, clip art, button graphics, line drawings, and all simpler, nonphotographic images work better as GIFs. Unlike JPGs, GIFs can be compressed without losing quality. Further, they can display only 256 colors per pixel, making them much more suitable for the Web. GIFs can be animated, interlaced, and made transparent. All of these effects can be created with more-advanced software such as Photoshop, Paint Shop Pro, and Fireworks.

Find It Online

At AOL Keyword: **Animated GIF** (or AOL Keyword: **AGIF**), you can download animated GIFs plus software to create such images. Many Web sites offer free animated GIFs you can download.

Optimizing Web Graphics: File Size

A picture's *size* on a Web page refers to the amount of space it takes up on the screen. Even a picture with low resolution can be made to fill a page. *Size* also refers to the number of pixels used to create the image and the resulting file size in kilobytes. The two are related; the more pixels in a file, the bigger the picture.

To reduce an image's size (in both senses), crop it to display only its essentials. After you've cropped an image, you can then reduce less-important color information. On the Web, you can display only 216 colors. Using a product like Adobe Photoshop, Macromedia Fireworks, or JASC Paint Shop Pro, you can apply this minimalist "Web safe" color palette to reduce file size.

Appendix B

Online Digital-Imaging Resources

Adobe Photoshop Tutorials

www.adobe.com/products/tips/photoshop.html

This official Adobe Photoshop site, shown in Figure B-1, focuses on the kind of specific tips that users of this high-end software crave, on topics such as using layers to improve unevenly lit photos, minimizing background noise, and making the most of Photoshop's selection tools. One tutorial even teaches you how to simulate the appearance of something that's on fire. The tutorials feature award-winning authors and experts in the field of graphic arts. Some of the tutorials are in QuickTime (video) format. For more Photoshop links, check out AOL Keyword: **Photoshop**.

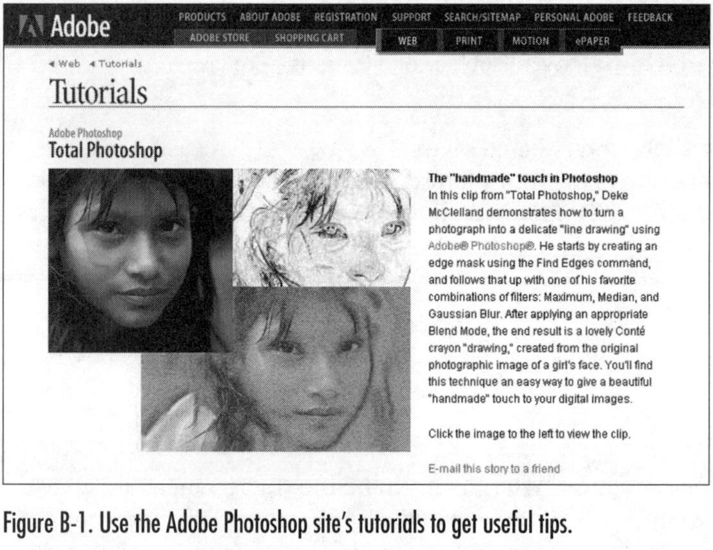

Figure B-1. Use the Adobe Photoshop site's tutorials to get useful tips.

AOL Decision Guides

AOL Keyword: **Personalogic**

Need a scanner, a printer, or a digital camera? Answer a few questions on the appropriate Personalogic-powered AOL Decision Guide, and the software identifies the equipment that best matches your needs. This guide even warns you if you have set your price too low or requirements too high. After you've identified a product, use AOL Keyword: **Shop@AOL** or **CNET** (Comparison Pricing) to find the best deal on the right product.

AOL Hometown: The Gallery

AOL Keyword: **Gallery**

`hometown.aol.com/hmtwnc9b/gallery.htm`

The Gallery showcases AOL members' pages featuring creative photography. Add it to your Favorite Places folder, because the topic attraction changes weekly. You can browse member's gallery pages as well as become a member of the Gallery yourself. Click the Gallery Web Boards link to read and post messages about using photographs in Web pages.

AOL Hometown: Photography Pages

AOL Keyword: **Hometown** (Hobbies and Interests⇨Creative Pursuits⇨Photography)

With a few clicks and a digital picture or two, you can easily create a Web site that shows off your pictures to the online world. The photography pages of AOL Hometown allow you to search for other members' work and to put your own photos online.

CNET

AOL Keyword: **CNET**

`www.cnet.com`

What can one say about what seems to be the (by far) most linked-to Web site dealing with all aspects of digital imaging? CNET, a creation of a cable network and the "anchor tenant" of AOL's Computing Channel, has impressive original content: in-depth product reviews, shoppers' guides, comparison pricing tables, how-to articles, and message boards, plus the browsing and searching features that make all of this content usable. Be patient, though, because with so much material the navigational paths are not always obvious, and some of the content is a year or two old.

Desktop Publishing Forum

AOL Keyword: **DTP** (AOL only)

Wondering what to do with your pictures once you have them in digital form? Check out AOL's Desktop Publishing Forum for in-depth information on all aspects of desktop publishing. In the reference center, you'll find a technical FAQ about scanning, originally published by the media coordinator at the University of Alabama's School of Medicine.

Digital Camera

AOL Keyword: **DPT** (AOL only)

Whereas AOL Keyword: **Photography** pulls together general photo areas on AOL and the Web, this AOL area has a narrower purpose: to introduce the benefits and features of digital cameras to AOL members and to suggest the kinds of activities possible with them.

Digital Photography

AOL Keyword: **Digital Photography** (AOL only)

> **Tip** In the Digital Photography Channel, under Digital Photo Tips & Tricks, you'll find a detailed summary of chats devoted to subjects such as preparing digital pictures for eBay (when you want to sell something).

This AOL "meta" area (it has lots of links to other sites) points you to diverse places on AOL and the Web where you can get help choosing a digital camera, learning how to use it, and sharing ideas and questions about digital cameras in the weekly digital photo chats. Check out the digital photo tips and tricks for some valuable tutorials.

Eastman Kodak Company

www.kodak.com

This large, searchable photography Web site makes you want to dust off your old 35mm camera. Learn how to take better pictures by exploring the Taking Great Pictures area. The Digital Learning Center contains ideas for activities for kids of different ages. Especially useful is the guide to dazzling array of new color films.

Graphic Arts

AOL Keyword: **Graphics** (AOL only)

This teeming AOL community offers a large set of graphics arts resources. Chat about or take a weekly online class about digital photography. Read or post messages on the digital photography message board. Click the software libraries and find downloadable software for whatever you need. Participate in a weekly graphic arts contest such as an Art Jam, where participants create collaborative slide shows by using all sorts of graphics in a sort of creative tag team!

How to Build Your Own Digital Darkroom

AOL Keyword: **Digital Darkroom** (AOL only)

This area is a must-visit if you're in the market for digital photography equipment. Another "meta site," Digital Darkroom provides a highly selective set of pointers to recent product reviews in CNET and stores like Beyond.com.

Image Exchange

AOL Keyword: **Image Exchange**

Caution: Look hard for copyright information at any Web site from which you want to download photos for use in your own work, whether it's for school or business. Make sure that you secure the necessary permissions before using any such images.

Double-click the Members Showcase folder to view digital images created by other AOL members. You can also easily upload your own images, too. The images are divided into categories such as photography, painting, pottery, and weaving.

Kodak: Digital Cameras and Technology

www.kodak.com/US/en/nav/digital.shtml

From advice on getting started in digital photography to ways to store and display your digital photographs, this comprehensive Web site offers information on just about everything you need to know about digital photography. This site also features links to Kodak products such as digital cameras and scanners. Be sure to visit the discussion forum, where you can ask a question or make a comment about digital photography.

Kodak Picture Playground

alts1.kodak.com/US/en/corp/playground/index.shtml

This is the fun epicenter of Kodak's large Web presence. Want to have a blast with your digital photos? Visit Kodak's Picture Playground and do simple digital-editing online. Upload your images from your computer and then reduce red eye or brighten up a dark picture. Turn pictures into puzzles or oil paintings, or apply special effects and make your boss look like a cartoon character.

National Geographic

www.nationalgeographic.com

The National Geographic Society, publishers of *National Geographic,* long known for its spectacular photography, has a site on the Web. Click the Photography link to see breathtaking photographs in the Visions Gallery. Enter a photography contest and learn some photography tips. A good place for kids, as well.

News and Photo Search

AOL Keyword: **News Search**

AOL provides an easy-to-use search engine that locates news articles and photographs. You can search all the categories or be more specific and choose a category such as business, sports, or entertainment. Or you can restrict your search to photographs. The help area gives tips on how to refine your search.

Online Classrooms

AOL Keyword: **Online Classroom**

AOL offers a variety of online classrooms, some of which cover graphic arts topics. These classrooms are often repeated weekly. For instance, the digital photography online classroom currently takes place Thursdays at 10:00 PM ET. When you find the class you want, double-click its title and choose Join Class.

Paint Shop Pro

AOL Keyword: **PSP**

Paint Shop Pro is a very popular imaging-editing program for Windows and is available in a shareware version. This AOL area gives some valuable tips for using the software. Download the shareware version here and then use the tutorial folder to learn how to use it. Discuss Paint Shop Pro in a chat or on the message boards. You may even want to participate in the weekly Paint Shop Pro Clinic.

Photographers on AOL

AOL Keyword: **Photographer**

This is the home for professional photographers on AOL. Learn about job opportunities, post a comment on the message boards, chat with fellow photographers in a weekly chat session, and learn where you can continue your education or attend seminars and or tradeshows.

Photography Forum

AOL Keyword: **Photography**

This Kodak-sponsored forum, part of the AOL Interests Channel, is a hub from which you can explore AOL and general photo resources on the Web. Take a poll concerning digital photography, or chat about the big issues as photography goes digital.

AOL's News Photos: Pictures of the Week and Picture of the Day

AOL Keyword: **News Photos** (AOL only); click a link to get the Pictures of the Week

AOL Keyword: **Pictures of the Week** features current photos in three categories: U.S. and World, Sports, and Entertainment. Most of the sites deal with up-to-the minute events. From AOL Keyword: **News Photos**, you can click to see Time.com photos and sports photos, and a single picture from the current day (or yesterday).

Popular Photography Online

AOL Keyword: **Pop Photo** (AOL only)

Tip

Want to share your photos with photo enthusiasts? Popular Photography Online gives you the chance to upload your photos and to view others' work.

This online version of *Popular Photography* magazine offers extensive and reliable information about photographic techniques and products. Learn about new talent in New Exposures, view spectacular photographs taken by professionals and amateurs in the Gallery, and check out new products in the Products Guide. You can also read or post messages on the message board.

Scanning

AOL Keyword: **Scanning** (AOL only)

Ever wondered what a TWAIN device actually does? Find out in the tutorials and tips folder of this Graphics Art area of the AOL Computing Channel. Find out how to use AOL to capture images from a digital camera or scanner. Also find out how to fix specific flaws in scans, such as color banding.

Taking the Long View: Panoramic Photographs

`lcweb2.loc.gov/ammem/pnhtml/pnhome.html`

This Library of Congress site is part of the American Memory Collection. It features sweeping panoramas dating from 1851–1991, including a portrait of the New York Giants (1905), a badly damaged

San Francisco after the earthquake (1906), a mostly rebuilt San Francisco (1914), and a 1914 panorama of the Elgin, Illinois watch factory. Browse the collection by subject, creator, or location, or search the collection by keyword.

Time-Life Photo Sight

`www.pathfinder.com/photo/index.html`

This Web site from Time, Inc., features photographs from the Time, Inc., photo collection (See Figure B-2). The photographs come from many of the magazines published by Time, Inc. including *Time, LIFE,* and *Sports Illustrated.* These photos are a great way to study the techniques of professional photographers. Each week a new Photo of the Week is featured. Be sure to take a look at the photo essays for some remarkable and memorable photographs.

Family outing, Birmingham, Alabama, 1956
Ed Clark/LIFE, copyright Time Inc.
RETURN TO GALLERY

Figure B-2. From Photo Sight's Popular Culture gallery, a family photo 1956-style.

"You've Got Pictures" Quick Start

AOL Keyword: **Pictures**

This handy guide answers your basic questions and gets you get started using "You've Got Pictures." For starters, you can locate your nearest participating developer by entering your zip code into the text box. Make sure to subscribe to a weekly newsletter about "You've Got Pictures" as well as browse the list of frequently asked questions.

INDEX

Numbers

A

B

C